D1242784

Robert Hall , Indian Fighter and Soldier

LIFE OF
ROBERT HALL

Indian Fighter and Veteran of Three Great Wars.

Also

Sketch of Big Foot Wallace

by
"Brazos"

STATE HOUSE PRESS
Austin, Texas
1992

Library of Congress Cataloging-in-Publication Data

Brazos.
Life of Robert Hall : Indian fighter and veteran of three great
wars : also Sketch of Big Foot Wallace / by Brazos ; new
introduction by Stephen L. Hardin.
p.   cm.
Originally published: Austin, Tex. : Ben C. Jones Printer,
1898.
Includes index.
ISBN 0-938349-89-9 (alk. paper)
ISBN 0-938349-90-2 (softcover : alk. paper)
ISBN 0-938349-91-0 (limited : alk. paper)
1. Hall, Robert, 1814-1899. 2. Pioneers—
Texas—Biography. 3. Texas Rangers—Biography
4. Texas—History—1846-1950. 5. Frontier and pioneer
life—Texas. 6. Indians of North America—Texas—Wars.
I. Title.

F391.H183B73 1992
976.4'061'092—dc20   92-28058
[B]

Printed in the United States of America

STATE HOUSE PRESS
P.O. Box 15247
Austin, Texas 78761

CONTENTS

ROBERT HALL: TEXIAN

"Any of us can command Texans. All they ask is to
be shown the road to the enemy's camp."

That accolade, attributed by Robert Hall to Texas Ranger
Captain John C. Hays, in many ways captures the essential
character of the frontier volunteer. Pioneer settler, Indian
fighter, Texas Ranger, and veteran of three wars, Hall spoke
with considerable authority. Although today largely forgotten,
few people in Texas history played a more combative role; Hall
appeared unable to pass up a fight. The list of his comrades in
those early struggles reads like an honor roll of early Texas
notables: Sam Houston, Edward Burleson, "Jack" Hays, Matthew "Old Paint" Caldwell, Ben McCulloch, Henry Mc-
Culloch, William "Bigfoot" Wallace, Felix Huston, Juan N.
Seguín, James Wilson Nichols, Cicero Rufus "Rufe" Perry,
James Kerr, Tom Green, and Creed Taylor. Indeed, Hall was
one of those stalwarts Hays lauded — a Lone Star warrior who
required only "to be shown the road to the enemy's camp."

"THE HARDIEST AND TOUGHEST OF BOYS"

Born in the Rocky River District of South Carolina, Robert was
one of the five children born to James and Rebecca Gassaway
Hall. Since his childhood was typical of that experienced by
most of the region's youngsters, his recollections provide rich
details of daily life that offer modern readers rare glimpses into
the social history of the antebellum South. Hall, for example,
recalled his "proudest and happiest day" as the one on which
he received a pair of "jeans pants":

They had been colored with copperas and the buttons were made of pieces of gourd covered with cloth. Although I was barefooted and had on a flax linen shirt, I would not have traded places with the President of the United States when I put on those pants.

In 1828 the Halls moved to Tennessee, where they threw up a cabin atop the Choctaw Bluffs in Memphis at the mouth of Wolf Creek. Later the family shifted to the Rutherford fork of the Obion River in Gibson County.

Obviously, Hall did not spring from the planter gentry, but from that rugged strain that Professor Frank Owsley classified as "plain folk." While lacking in numerous creature comforts, these open-hearted people were more than willing to extend traditional southern hospitality. To deny a traveler the comfort of one's home was considered unneighborly, unsouthern, and downright unchristian. Hall recalled that his "Hard-Shell" Baptist congregation would routinely "turn people out of the church for refusing to keep strangers over night."

Yet the same southerner who offered a stranger a bed for the night might easily maim him the following morning for some imagined slight. Hall makes it clear that the South of his youth was a violent locale. During his stint as a flatboatman, he fell in with "a hard set" and learned to be quick with his wits and his fists. Life on the river produced numerous "ring-tailed squealers" like Mike Fink, the legendary "King of the Keelboatmen," whom David Crockett reportedly regarded as a "helliferocious fellow." Hall introduces us to similar characters, such as the "desperado by the name of Phelps"—a boisterous delinquent who bragged "a bowie knife was his looking glass, and a pistol shot was soothing to his soul."

Of all the rogues Hall encountered along the river, the most "desperate character" was probably John A. Murrell. Although one of the most notorious criminals of his day, he is now omitted from history texts. Murrell led an outlaw gang that boasted more than a thousand members whose activities ranged over eight states of the Old Southwest. Slave-stealing became Murrell's specialty. He would entice a bondsman away from his master with promises of freedom, only to sell him downriver to an unsuspecting buyer. Murrell then stole the slave again and repeated the process until posters describing the runaway appeared up and down the river. Murrell would then murder the slave and sink the body; dead men could provide no evidence against him. In the early 1830s, rivermen and townfolk alike were outraged when particulars of the so-called "Murrell Conspiracy" came to light—he allegedly intended to raise an army of runaway slaves and white riff-raff and take over the entire region. When Arkansas lawmen captured Murrell and put him away in 1834, his nefarious scheme fell apart.

In the company of such rogues it was only natural that Hall would have been involved in numerous life-threatening scrapes. Yet, as he tells it, many more were of a recreational nature. On the old southwestern frontier two local toughs might fight it out simply to determine the "He-bull" of the neighborhood. These were no-holds-barred affairs; eye-gouging, ear-pulling and nose-biting all fell within the bounds of accepted practice. During his set-to with Louis Witherbry, Hall relates that he "bit nine pieces out of his back."

Anglo-Celtic southerners clearly enjoyed a good brawl. In times of war they were eager to pit their long rifles against the enemy; in times of peace, they fought each other. As law crept into the backwoods, many resented the infringement of their "liberty" and sought new frontiers that demonstrated a higher tolerance of their rough-and-rowdy folkways. One American brought up on manslaughter charges bitterly complained:

> Now-a-days you can't put an inch or so of knife into
> a fellow, or lam him over the head with a stick of
> wood, but every little lacky must poke his nose in,
> and law, law, law, is the word . . . . I tell you I won't

stay in no such country. I mean to go to Texas, where a man can have some peace and not be interfered with in his private concerns.

Still, not all of Hall's acquaintances were miscreants. His anecdotes concerning David Crockett are not only delightful, but constitute a source that students of the Tennessee congressman and Alamo hero have generally overlooked. Even as Hall unabashedly describes gnawing nine pieces out of a man's back, he reveals pangs of conscious about casting an illegal vote for Crockett at the tender age of eighteen—in his day, the legal voting age was still twenty-one. As Hall told it, Crockett was "present at every frolic, log rolling, or house raising." Consequently, his neighbors remembered him as "one of the most popular men that ever lived." Crockett never forgot his frontier roots; he may have been a congressman in Washington but when he returned home he "took his liquor out of a gourd."

"IN THE CAUSE OF TEXAS"

In the spring of 1836 Hall joined a group of Kentucky volunteers bound for Texas. They were eager to assist the Texians in their rebellion against the dictatorial regime of Antonio López de Santa Anna. By the time they arrived, however, the battle of San Jacinto had been won, Santa Anna taken prisoner, and the Mexican Army was in full retreat. Nevertheless, Texas commanders anticipated that once the Mexicans had regrouped they would mount another campaign to reclaim the fledgling republic. Hall joined the Army of the Republic on June 1, 1836, and was subsequently stationed at Camp Johnson on the Lavaca River. Hall was mistaken when he claimed the camp was named after Albert Sidney Johnston; this camp, founded in September, 1836, appears to have been named for Francis W. Johnson, one of the leaders of the 1835 storming of Bexar. It was a natural mistake; a Camp Johnston existed, which was named for the future Confederate general, but it was located in southwestern Smith County and not established until 1839.

He recalled all too vividly, however, the dangers and drudgery of camp life. Dysentery swept the Texian garrison and more than "300 brave fellows were wrapped in their blankets and laid away in the earth of that camp." Had it not been for the careful nursing of a solicitous comrade, Hall himself would have fallen victim to the malady. The men lacked almost every item required for life in the field. They existed almost exclusively on local beef; Hall lamented that during his four-month stint he "never saw a piece of bread." Southern boys raised on cornbread and buttermilk found the all-beef diet unappetizing. "The best of us," Hall avowed, "would have traded our interest in the fortune of the Lone Star Republic for a good big skillet of cornbread." The restless Hall discovered the lot of a regular soldier was not what he had expected. "I was awful weak (from his bout with dysentery)," he asserted, "and getting awful sick of the inactivity and hardship of army life." After bribing an army physician, he received a medical discharge on November 7, 1836, and rushed to Columbia to reacquaint himself with civilian fare. But before reaching that settlement he literally sniffed out a churn of buttermilk and quaffed down amounts sufficient to "kill an ordinary man."

Footloose with few prospects, Hall toyed with the idea of returning to the United States, but the affections of a pretty girl were to bind his destiny to Texas. He made his way to Montgomery County where he sharecropped, but his mind was not totally occupied with agricultural pursuits. Colonel John G. King boasted "three of the prettiest girls in Texas," and Hall set out to claim one for his bride. Decked out in his best suit, he boldly rode to the colonel's residence where his "heart was at once captured" by the lovely Mary Minerva "Polly" King. The lady responded to the attentions of this dashing swain and on June 20, 1837, District Judge James W. Robinson joined the couple in wedlock. Their marriage license was issued and recorded in Gonzales County May 31, 1838; at that time there may have been another ceremony for Hall claimed to have married Polly twice. The union was to last forty-three years and produce thirteen children.

During the Runaway Scrape of 1836 Colonel King had removed his family from the Gonzales area where he had lived several years prior to the revolution. A son, William P. King, perished at the Alamo. After the war King wanted to reclaim his land near Gonzales but was wary that Indians had taken possession of the western frontier. With his new son-in-law in tow, he returned to reconnoiter his homestead. The pair found the town of Gonzales in charred ruins but, remarkably, the corn crop remained intact. Late in the autumn of 1837, King and Hall were "pretty certain" that the threat of Mexican invasion had passed and moved their families back to the desolated area. Hall was eager to make a real home for himself and his new bride, yet Comanches remained a constant menace. For men like Hall, fighting Indians was merely one of the chores of frontier life. "We built a little log fort, he recounted, "and prepared to settle down for life."

Eager to protect his new home, Hall joined Matthew Caldwell's ranger company and was elected second lieutenant. Hall found service with the rangers better suited to his temperament than the regular army. Rangers only mustered for a real crisis; there was none of the "hurry up and wait" of garrison duty. In 1838 Hall and another thirty-three rangers of Caldwell's company laid out the settlement of Walnut Springs; Ben McCulloch surveyed the town. They subsequently discovered that another community had registered the name Walnut Springs and changed the name of their new village to Seguin, after the *tejano* hero Juan Nepomuceno Seguín. The fledgling hamlet subsequently became the county seat of Guadalupe County.

But establishing towns was not a ranger's primary responsibility. In October 1838, Comanches raided into the settlement and kidnapped Matilda Lockhart, daughter of Andrew Lockhart, and four children of Mitchell Putnam. Caldwell's rangers pursued the raiders to their camp, but in the face of overwhelming numbers could not rescue the captive children. Even as an old man, Hall expressed his frustration at being unable to adequately defend women and children against the forays of Comanche marauders: "It was a matter of great regret with the frontier settlers that we were not strong enough to fight the red devils who held the two young ladies and several children captive." This was an all too common lament, especially before the arming of the Texas Rangers with the Patterson Colt revolver.

As he gained experience as an Indian fighter, Hall was careful to observe their customs and habits. He made an effort to cultivate and understand friendly Indians like the Lipans and Tonkawas, who on several occasions proved useful allies against the implacable Comanches. Unlike many of the old Texians, Hall eschewed the "only-good-Indian-a-dead Indian" canard and noted the honesty, courage, and loyalty of the Lipans, whom he described as "the most faithful of allies and the most terrible of foes."

In August 1840, Hall fought at Plum Creek, an action which one authority characterized as "one of the most significant Indian battles of Texas history." The encounter was not only decisive, it was also one of the most widely reported. Numerous participants such as Z. N. Morrell, John H. Jenkins, John Henry Brown, James Wilson Nichols, and J. W. Wilbarger all left narratives recounting their experiences during the Great Comanche Raid. Yet, because it is so rare, Hall's account is regrettably seldom cited in the literature of the campaign. Hall, who was wounded during the engagement, provides a gritty, intense chronicle, rich with perspective that only one who has looked his enemy in the eye can provide: "I fired right in the Indian's face and knocked him off his horse, but did not kill him. However, I got the fine hat he had stolen."

Hall, who learned only too well the toils and dangers of frontier life, exhibited both amazement and pride at the fortitude of Texas women. "No pen will ever be able to do justice to the courage, patriotism, and devotion of the women who stood by their brothers, fathers, husbands, and sweethearts, while they were repelling the Mexicans, destroying the Indians, killing the snakes, and building the roads in the wilderness of Texas." Hall regretted the sacrifices his Polly had been forced to make and lamented that her travails "hurt me very badly." Unlike many Texas men, he demonstrated an uncommon sensitivity to her comfort and took extraordinary pains to provide her with the "little things to please a woman's heart." One of the most poignant of Hall's anecdotes relates his two hundred mile jaunt through Indian infested country to secure Polly a new dress. She implored him not to go, but Hall assured her that he "had a good horse and a good gun" and would not be deterred by hostiles. For Texians of Hall's ilk, a fast horse and a true rifle were all they required.

Although frontier life provided its full share of hardships, there were also occasional moments of levity. One of Hall's neighbors, James Wilson Nichols, told of the time he pitted his mustang against "a noted race horse" belonging to "Bob" Hall. The wager was five dollars, one which Nichols apparently won. Hall does not mention it, but the "noted race horse" was probably the "good horse" he rode to buy Polly's new dress and the "fine race mare" he would take to war in Mexco.

"THE PROSE OF WAR"

In 1845 the annexation of Texas to the United States instigated further conflict with Mexico. Hall opposed the union, having "voted first, last, and always for the Lone Star." Yet, true to character, he joined a local ranger company and rode southward to join the army of General Zachary Taylor. Hall's recollections of his activities with the Texas Rangers in Mexico complement better known primary accounts such as Samuel C. Reid's 1848 book *The Scouting Expeditions of McCulloch's Texas Rangers.*

Stopping in San Antonio, Hall spent twenty-five dollars—a considerable sum at the time—for "the finest bowie knife [he] ever saw." Having often fought Mexican irregulars, he knew their favorite tactic was to lasso an enemy, then drag him to death — a prospect Hall did not relish. He, therefore, secured his new knife under his shirt so that it would be accessible to cut the rope in case he were snared in the lethal noose of an enemy *ranchero.*

The blade was passed down to Hall's descendants and was part of the collection placed on display for the 1936 Centennial celebrations. The Dallas Historical Society maintained the Hall collection until 1983, when William R. Strobel reclaimed it for the family. At that time, the DHS staff could not locate the knife and it was presumed stolen.

On February 23, 1847, Hall participated in the pivotal battle of Buena Vista, in which General Taylor's mixed-bag of five thousand regulars and state militia met and matched General Santa Anna's army of eighteen thousand. Hall possessed a highly selective memory and did not attempt to detail every aspect of the battle, but rather recalled those episodes that made specific impressions on him. Again, the rarity of the 1898 edition of the *Life of Robert Hall* has caused it to be omitted from most bibliographies of the Mexican War.

Even more moving than Hall's stories of the battle is his eerie description of its aftermath. Santa Anna retreated in such haste that he left a trail of dead and wounded in his wake. By the rules of civilized warfare, American surgeons tended the enemy wounded. Hall was astounded by the haste and apparent nonchalance with which they performed numerous amputations: "The doctors had a great knife like a carving knife. They would make the peons throw the poor wounded devils on a big box, and they would slash off the legs and arms as if they were in the butcher business." The scene Hall recounts is almost surreal: the field is littered with bags of beans jettisoned by routed Mexicans; the wounded moan; looters strip the dead and dying; wounded horses roam aimlessly; severed hands and feet clutter a disabled ambulance.

As McCulloch's rangers pressed the enemy's withdrawal, they repeatedly encountered groups of wounded *soldados*, abandoned to the mercy of the Americans. Almost every dwelling along the route was "jammed with wounded." Tragically, one building caught fire and a number of the immobile casualties were burned to death. Even years later, Hall could not recount the heart-rending events of the pursuit following Buena Vista without betraying emotion. "Such," he observed, "is the prose of war."

It was during the pursuit of the retreating Mexican Army that Hall acquired a treasured war souvenir. Near the town of Encarnación, Hall spied a suspicious Mexican civilian mount his horse and bolt away. Hall, astride a "fine race mare," quickly overtook the suspect and confiscated his purse containing $333.00 in silver, a valuable cloak, and a "fine sword." From the sword's appearance, he had just cause to be wary of it owner. It was not the lengthy regulation blade of the line cavalrymen; it instead closely resembled the short-bladed *espada ancha* favored by the dreaded *guerrilleros*. His commanding officer insisted that Hall return the cloak, but he retained possession of the silver and the weapon; as an old man he boasted, "I have the sword yet."

The sword remained with Hall's descendants until 1958, when his granddaughter, Mrs. George Miller of San Antonio, donated it to the Seguin Conservation Society for placement in its Los Nogales Museum. By 1990 dust and grime had taken their toll on the weapon. That year Robert's great-grandson, John Hall of San Antonio, borrowed the blade and restored it to its original luster. Along with its leather sheath, the exquisite, silver-mounted sword is again on display at the Los Nogales Museum.

"REST AND PEACE?"

In 1850 the Hall family lived on Sandies Creek in Gonzales County. Robert painted an idylic portrait of the years between the wars. "We were congratulating ourselves that we had the finest country on earth," he pronounced, "and that it would be easy for us to transmit large landed estates and plenty of cattle and horses to our children."

Nevertheless, the Halls spent much of that time embroiled in legal wrangles. In 1856 Robert joined Polly in bringing suit against John Loyd, Henry Trammell, and Harrison Askey of Gonzales County; John Baker and Alfred Bailes of Guadalupe County; and Creed Taylor of Bexar County. The Halls alleged that on or about December 10, 1854, the defendants had absconded with ninety-five head of cattle, the "separate property of Mary Hall." To support their claim, the Halls introduced an 1831 register of the PK (Polly King) brand. In addition, they provided a schedule of Polly's separate property recorded in September, 1848, which listed 180 head of cattle marked with her PK brand.

Although Baker had died, the other defendants vigorously denied the charges. Testimony revealed that both Halls had signed a promissory note for one hundred head of Robert's cattle as a bet in a horse race with Askey. When Askey's horse won, he sold the promissory note to Creed Taylor of Bexar County. Taylor was not a man to be trifled with. A hard-boiled frontiersman, he was a veteran of the Texas Revolution and would emerge as the patriarch of one of the factions in the notorious Sutton-Taylor feud. Taylor asserted that his co-defendants were "not concerned at all" in the removal of the cattle, but had only been named for the purpose of having the case tried within the jurisdiction of the Gonzales County Court. Taylor further testified that he had confronted the Halls, explained his arrangement with Askey, and both Robert and Polly had instructed him to "gather the said stock himself."

Taylor admitted to rounding up and driving off eighty-six head, which were "all he could find."

A witness, W.D. Smith, testified that most of the cattle that Taylor had collected bore Polly's brand. The plaintiffs argued that since the cattle in question bore Polly's distinctive PK brand, they could reasonably be considered part of Robert's herd. The jury found for the plaintiffs against Taylor, but declared the other defendants not guilty.

Legal problems continued to plague the Halls. In 1845 the Republic of Texas awarded Robert two labors of land for his military service, which was recorded on Book C, page 608 of the deed records of Guadalupe County. In 1857, however, the Supreme Court of Texas awarded the land to Sterling Pearson as part of a decision in a law suit he had brought against Hall. Even so, Robert kept the family in the area, for the 1860 census listed Robert, Polly, and their ten children residing on the banks of the Guadalupe River.

"FRATRICIDAL STRUGGLE"

Hall joined Confederate ranks with a wistful heart. A Unionist, he had opposed both slavery and secession. "It was a terror," he asserted, "to be torn from the flag I had been born under, and which I had fought under." Well into middle age, Hall could have easily remained at home; yet, like many Texans, he could not remain idle while his state marched to war. After much soul searching he resolved "there was nothing left for us to do but shoulder arms and join our old comrades."

Despite extensive combat experience and his advanced age, Hall served as an enlisted man throughout the war. On May 31, 1862, he mustered into service at a camp on the Salado River, joining Colonel Peter C. Wood's 36th Texas Cavalry Regiment; Nat Benton served as lieutenant colonel and William 0. Hutchison as major. Hall fell in with his brother-in-law's company. Enjoying the fellowship of friends and family, he recalled "we drank a good deal of whisky in that camp."

For nearly a year the 36th Texas Cavalry "scouted about" on the western frontier. That assignment appears not to have left much of an impression upon Hall, for he relegates it to only a passing mention.

Hotter action was brewing along the Texas Gulf Coast. Texans boasted that during the war Yankees were never able to invade Texas; it was nonetheless true that the Union Navy blockaded and occupied several of the state's most important ports. In the waning months of 1863, the 36th rode to Calhoun County, where they resisted Union efforts to capture Matagorda Island. While recounting this action, Hall's memory faltered slightly. There is no record of a "Fort Saluria," but Fort Esperanza was indeed located near the coastal community of Saluria. When enemy occupation appeared imminent, most noncombatants fled to the mainland, but a battalion of Confederate artillery defended both the post and the village until November 29, 1863, when it also withdrew to the mainland. The retreating rebels blew up the lighthouse, dismantled the fort, and burned the town. Shortly thereafter, Matagorda Island was occupied by Federal troops under General Nathaniel P. Banks. Hall reported that following the capture of the island, his regiment withdrew up the coastline to pitch camp at "Old Caney," at other times called "Caney Crossing," or Caney Creek, an old bed of the Colorado River in Matagorda County.

The 36th Texas Cavalry had not seen the last of their adversary, Nathaniel P. Banks. By March 1864, he had taken command of some 27,000 Federal troops assembled for an invasion of Texas by way of the Red River. The invasion force was supported by a flotilla of gunboats under Rear Admiral David D. Porter. Boasting an apparently overwhelming superiority of men and material, Banks anticipated crushing any Confederate resistance, capturing Shreveport, and driving into Texas. The 36th Texas Cavalry transferred to Louisiana to confront the new threat. General Edmund Kirby Smith concentrated his meager Confederate army at Shreveport and directed Major General Richard Taylor to oppose Banks with his force of 11,000, including numerous Texas units. On April 8, 1864, at the head of some 8,800 Confederates, Taylor attacked the Federal vanguard of about 8,000 near Mansfield, some fifty miles south of Shreveport. Taylor's bold counterstroke caught the Federals completely unprepared and he trounced their vanguard, killing almost one thousand invaders and capturing 2,500 prisoners, 22 pieces of ordnance, and 150 supply wagons. The following day, however, Confederates pursuing retreating Yankees were badly mauled, suffering about 1,500 casualties at Pleasant Hill. Nevertheless, that night Banks withdrew under the cover of darkness. The two days of fighting at Mansfield and Pleasant Hill had successfully thwarted Union plans to invade Texas.

The 36th Texas Cavalry did not arrive in time to fight at Mansfield and Pleasant Hill. Yet, as General Banks withdrew his force, Hall laconically remarked: "We followed." Banks directed Porter to withdraw his fleet, but the shallow water, narrow channels, and hair-pin turns of the Red River made turning about extremely difficult. General Tayor saw an opportunity to intercept and capture the entire enemy flotilla. On April 12, Texas troops under Brigadier General Thomas Green located two Federal gunboats which had run aground in midstream. Green ordered Wood's regiment dismounted and placed the unit on the rebel right. Hall and his comrades pressed forward "with a true rebel yell" toward the river bank in front of the enemy's seemingly helpless vessels.

A Union officer aboard the *Osage* described the scene: "Then commenced one of the most curious fights of the war, 2,500 infantry against a gunboat aground." The boats were not as impotent as they appeared. Union gunners opened their ports and blasted the charging Confederates. One Johnny Reb bitterly recalled "shells bursting around, solid shot ploughing the ground, grape, cannister and minnie balls whistling through the ranks." Yet the men in gray pressed ahead. In his official report one Union officer recorded, "The rebels fought with unusual pertinacity for over an hour, delivering the heaviest and most concentrated fire of musketry that I have ever witnessed." In the forefront of action, General Green was killed in an especially gruesome—albeit quick—manner when a round shot all but took off his head. In the face of such withering fire and demoralized by the death of Green, the Confederates were finally compelled to withdraw.

Banks and Porter continued to retreat as the Confederate forces snapped at their rear. The fight of Jenkins's Ferry, on April 30, essentially concluded Banks's abortive Red River Campaign. Hall participated in numerous skirmishes during the pursuit. True to pattern, he never attempted to recount grand strategy, but rather offered the enlisted man's worm's eye view of the fighting. An older and wiser soldier, Hall did not engage in the kind of reckless heroics that he had demonstrated in his youth. Chapter XXIII expresses little of the bravado of the earlier narrative; instead, proclamations of fright, fatigue, and misgivings prevail.

Hall may have questioned the wisdom of the war, but during its course he developed a lasting loathing for Yankees. "The Federal army left desolation and smoking ruins in their wake," he lamented. "No Comanches, in their raids in Texas, had ever butchered, plundered, murdered, and burned as the Federals did on their retreat." Hall expressed a special enmity toward General Banks, whom he castigated as the "Comanche of the Federal Army." As Hall told it, Banks "burned every town, every house and everything that he could possibly destroy in his mad retreat." Capping that denunciation, Hall posed the rhetorical question: "Will history dare to call such a monster of iniquity and imbecility a general?"

Hall was sickened by the needless waste of life and property. An 1864 report recorded that on February 1, Hall was in "pursuit of deserters." At some point shortly thereafter he received a furlough to return home and his narrative seems to suggest that, like thousands of other southern soldiers, he simply failed to return to the fighting. Unlike many of his contemporaries who advanced sentimental notions of the "Lost Cause," Hall harbored no illusions concerning what he considered a national tragedy:

> It was a war I did not like, nor do I like to write of my service in it. Let it suffice for my decendants to know that I served as a soldier in that great war, and did my duty as a soldier, as I did in all other wars. That will be enough for them to remember of me in that fratricidal struggle.

"AN HONORABLE AND WORTHY OLD MAN"

Returning home from the war, Hall did not long enjoy domestic tranquility; for in 1866 he once again found himself in court—again as the defendant. In 1861 he and Polly had consigned a $364.00 note, payable within one year's time, for goods received from B. B. Peck & Company, a Gonzales general store. The partners of the firm apparently made no effort to receive payment while Hall served in the army; given the sorry condition of Texas's war-ruined economy they must have realized what a fruitless effort that would prove. Yet with an able-bodied Hall back home, William D. W. Peck, the surviving partner, believed he had a right to expect payment and brought suit against Robert and Polly.

The couple once again used the separation of property defence that they had employed in 1856. Polly avowed that she "never made any contract with B. B. Peck." She admitted she had consigned the note, but testified that she "did not do it of my own good, free will" and that she had used few of the goods in question: "I have examined the bill of items annexed to this interrogatory, and remember but little about it. I suppose I purchased a few of the articles mentioned in the bill, but very few. The greater part I know nothing about. The articles I did purchase were actually necessary for myself and family." Such being the case, she believed the bill ought not to be paid with her money. Robert, on the other hand, simply had no money of his own. The jury did not accept this somewhat tenuous line of reasoning and found for the plaintiff.

Some articles on the itemized bill rebuff the portrait of the sparse and rugged frontier existence that Robert paints in his memoirs; included among the other household items are: a "Fancy silk Cravat," a "Fancy check Tie," a "Fine Silk Vest," and "Doe Skin Pants."

Shortly following that decision, Robert moved the family to South Texas where he drove cattle in the brush country along the Nueces River. Later he settled in Dimmit County, on the Indian Bend of the river at Rock Crossing between Carrizo Springs and Cotulla. During the war few of the cattle had been marked or branded and, according to Hall, "herds had increased wonderfully." Feral stock, those local *tejanos* called *los mesteños,* were rife throughout the area. So common, in fact, that "it became a common thing for a man to go out and brand these wild cattle and kill a calf whenever they [*sic*] wanted it."

During the 1870s Robert became an active member of the Texas Veterans Association and the records of that organization indicate his attendance at several of the annual meetings. The April 12, 1879, issue of the Gonzales *Inquirer* noted the visit of one of the town's original settlers:

> Mr. Robert Hall, an aged Texas veteran on his way to the reunion of Texas veterans at Galveston, called to see us Thursday. He is familiar with early scenes around Gonzales. He is now living on the Nueces river, in McMullen county, but is preparing to move to Dimmit, an unorganized county. He related to us many interesting incidents in connection with his life in the west. The leopard we spoke of some time since

was captured by his sons. After exhibiting it at Austin he sold it to Forepaugh's circus. Panthers, wild cats, leopards, Mexican lions, jaguars, etc., he tells us, abound in the Nueces bottom.

On their way home from the Galveston meeting, the Halls spent more time in Gonzales; on April 26, the *Inquirer* again noted their visit.

> Mr. Robert Hall, better known as "old Ranger Bob," called to see us this week. He says he received from Moses Austin Bryan a certificate of membership for himself and wife in the Texas veteran association, and started down to the last reunion. Taking the train at Luling, on the Sunset route, the conductor allowed Mr. Hall his ticket, but would not give one to Mrs. Hall. Mr. Hall seemed to think this pretty rough treatment. They had traveled a long way, and believed themselves entitled to a ticket.

Hall savored his role as the venerable old veteran and, as the above report indicates, attempted to exploit it to the hilt. During the 1870s, long after his Indian fighting days, Hall concocted a dazzling buckskin costume adorned with a wild assortment of animal pelts, which he never tired of wearing on "gala days and at the gathering of the old veterans." Lavishly embroidered, his "magnificent frontiersman's suit" was pure public relations. As early as the 1830s the image of the buck-skin-clad, fur-cap-bedecked backwoodsman had captured the American imagination. Toward the end of his career, David Crockett began to appear in public dressed in hunting garb to bolster his growing persona as the "Lion of the West," although his preference for more conventional "gentleman's" clothing is well documented. Likewise, Hall appeared in his outlandish ensemble to fulfill the public's expectations of what an old Texas pioneer should look like. Nevertheless, earlier photographs reveal that Hall did not routinely don buckskins to perform his daily chores. Like many old-timers, he was an active participant in the creation of the sartorial frontier stereotype.

In fact, the "frontiersman's suit" outlived Hall. While collecting historic costumes for the 1936 Texas Centennial Exposition, Mary Reid acquired Hall's attire. In 1942 she explained the outfit "included trousers, coat, and a vest all of fringed and beaded buckskins. Once there had been a coonskin cap, but the moths long ago had made a feast of it." Reid further described various other items that Hall had owned: "There was a Bowie knife and a leather-covered canteen. A powder horn carved to resemble a fish with the words, El Pirata, in the design carried the story that it had originally belonged to [Jean] Lafitte, who gave it to Mrs. Jane Long, who in turn presented it to General Sam Houston, who in turn gave it to Robert Hall, one of the guards of Santa Anna after the Battle of San Jacinto."

Another Texas notable momentarily sported Hall's apparel. In 1936 the respected Texas historian Herbert P. Gambrell served as the director of historical exhibits for the Texas Centennial Exposition. Mary Reid mentioned in passing that Hall had stood six feet four inches tall. Ever the skeptic, Dr. Gambrell—himself a robust man—inquired, "What is your authority for that statement? Every pioneer Texan was six feet four inches if we are to believe all the tall tales." Reid replied that she had never actually seen Hall but invited Gambrell to note the size of the garments. "When the director saw it there was a gleam in his eye," Reid recounted, "and he hurried me in his office with the admonition to let no one in. In a few minutes the door opened and out walked Mr. Gambrell in Robert Hall's buckskin suit, the powder horn slung over his shoulder." The young woman could not resist a slight dig at the director; "Well, what do you think about Robert Hall now?" she asked. "I think," the master replied, "that he was quite a man." The garments and accompanying items were housed at the Dallas Historical Society until William R. Strobel, a Hall descendent, reclaimed them in 1983. He passed on the "extraordinary wearing apparel" to his son who currently resides in Colorado.

Hall's beloved Polly died in Carrizo Springs on December 12, 1880. Her body was temporarily buried on the ranch at Rock Crossing before it was reinterred in the King family cemetery near Belmont in Gonzales County. Crushed by sorrow, Robert acknowledged that for a period he "became a wild man." Following a period of intense mourning, Hall came to terms with his grief and pursued numerous interests. Although money was tight, he managed to scrape together enough to travel to many of the annual meetings of the Texas Veterans Association. In September 1893 he visited friends and relatives in Gonzales. Hall seemed to have suffered few of the afflictions of advanced years. "Mr. Hall is an old Texas veteran of the first water," a local journalist reported. "He is 82 years of age and is hale and hearty. . . . The desire for hunting and roaming the prairies still attracts him, which he indulges in occasionally on the Nueces . . . . Mr. Hall is an interesting man and delights a listener with his experiences."

The old man spent the last years of his life living with his children in Cotulla, surrounded by his grandchildren and respected in the community. He devoted a portion of that time dictating his memoirs and working with Ben C. Jones Press in Austin to have a number of copies printed. On December 19, 1899, the old warrior died in Cotulla. Two day later the Gonzales *Inquirer* announced the woeful news:

> A telephone message was received this morning by Mr. J. W. Ramsay stating that Mr. Robert Hall was dead. He died Tuesday at his home in Cotulla. His remains arrived last night at Luling and he will be taken tomorrow, Friday, to the King burying ground near Oak Forest for interment by the side of his wife. Several of his relatives and old friends in Gonzales will attend the funeral. Mr. Hall was 87 years of age. He was born in South Carolina and came to Texas and enlisted in Sam Houston's army just after the

battle of San Jacinto. He also served in the Mexican war and with the republic troops fighting the Indians and had many adventures in the early days. He came to Gonzales and married on the 20 of June, 1837, Miss Pollie King, daughter of Colonel John G. King, then living near Gonzales. He leaves several children living in West Texas. For the past fifteen years Mr. Hall has been living at Cotulla. Mr. Hall was an interesting character and was a typical old pioneer and frontiersman. He visited several cities of the state and frequently wore his old Indian uniform. He was an honorable and worthy old man.

LIFE OF ROBERT HALL

In the book trade, "rare" is a designation that is frequently misused. Yet, in regard to *Life of Robert Hall* that term may be applied without reservation. Indeed, Texana dealers and collectors consider it one of the rarest and coveted of titles. Austin book dealer Ray Walton, who has spent more than thirty years in the trade, reports that the volume has passed through his hands only once. He further observes that if a copy were available for sale, a conservative estimate of its value would be $2,500. The book is seldom to be found in even the largest repositories. The Barker Texas History Center at The University of Texas at Austin boasts two copies, the Daughters of the Republic of Texas Library at the Alamo owns one in extremely fragile condition; the Texas State Library used to have a copy, but it has "disappeared" from their stacks.

According to "Brazos," the editor, the volume was compiled after interviews with both Robert Hall and William "Bigfoot" Wallace. Yet the Hall material is vastly superior to the small Wallace chapter, which looks to have been included as an afterthought. After extensive research, the identity of "Brazos" remains an enigma. One of Hall's descendants believes that

"Brazos" was a family member, and considering the intimate nature of the narrative that is entirely possible. In a 1967 letter to University of Texas Librarian Llerena Friend, Harry Williamson, a nephew of Hall's, expressed his belief that the book "is in reality an autobiograhy [*sic*] of my Uncle Bob." Hall, however, was no man of letters and it is unlikely that he wrote the book himself. Nevertheless, it is almost certain that he was an active participant in its preparation and printing.

Given the book's publishing history, it is not surprising that it is so rare. The manuscript was set in type by the Austin job printing firm of Ben C. Jones & Company. It appears odd that Hall, or "Brazos," would have employed a press so far from Cotulla. Still, Jones had established a reputation for printing historical subjects, which may have influenced the decision. At the time the firm printed the *Quarterly of the Texas Historical Association,* and advertised in its pages; two years after it produced Hall's book, the firm printed Andrew Jackson Sowell's classic, *Early Settlers and Indian Fighters of Southwest Texas.* It should be noted, however, that Ben C. Jones & Company was a press, not a publisher. Once the job was in print, it was the customer's responsibility to sell it. The fact that *Life of Robert Hall* was never advertised for sale nor reviewed in historical journals suggests the book was given to family members and close friends. In all likelihood, the first and only print run numbered less than a thousand.

The book's binding was not conducive to a long shelf life. It was bound in paper wrappers and printed on highly acidic paper. A photograph of Hall decked out in his frontiersman's costume appeared on the front cover, while the back cover featured a rear view of the same pose. The wrappers were issued in both olive green and dark blue, and perhaps even more colors, but those are the only two which appear on the few remaining copies.

Can readers rely that everything in *Life of Robert Hall* is the gospel truth? Absolutely not. Like all sources, it should be used judiciously. One may reliably assert that Hall's narrative is no better or worse than most old soldier memoirs. A practitioner of a time-honored frontier tradition, Hall was part of the breed that folklorist J. Frank Dobie characterized as "authentic liars." According to Dobie, such a rascal "may lie with satiric intent; he may lie merely to make the time pass pleasantly; he may lie in order to take the wind out of some egotistic fellow of his own tribe or to take in some greener; again, without any purpose at all and directed only by his ebullient and companion-loving nature, he may 'stretch the blanket' merely because, like the redoubtable Tom Ochiltree, he had 'rather lie on credit than tell the truth for cash.' His generous nature revolts at the monotony of everyday facts and overflows with desire to make his company joyful." To be sure, Hall included some dubious episodes to season his narrative. Fortunately, they are so outrageous there is no way one can mistake them as anything else. Stories of killing two bucks with one shot and the catfish whose hide was so tough it snapped a bayonet are clearly "whoppers." It is equally obvious that Hall intended them to be read as such. Yet one should not be too eager to dismiss elements of Hall's narrative that appear incredible — many are corroborated by contemporary sources.

Modern readers are likely to be surprised—perhaps repelled—by Hall's lack of modesty. Throughout the narrative he described himself in grandly hyperbolic terms: "I was . . . one of the wildest and most consummate young scamps in all America"; "I had a heart of gold and the courage of a dozen lions"; "I am sure that under fire I was just as cool and undisturbed as Junot or Lannes." Even in the Lone Star State, where the "Texas Brag" achieved epic proportions, those who brandish their own abilities are nowadays regarded as self-absorbed boors. As Professor Joseph Leach explained it, however, "virile behavior and a bragging manner, characteristic of any people during their heroic age, had been basic in the American personality from the first settling of the frontier." In words that could apply specifically to Hall, Dr. Leach continues:

> Where the bare necessities of life came hard, a man's physical abilities counted for almost everything. Superior fighting prowess was universally admired. The frontiersman who could hold his own against such usual adversaries as floods and storms, bears and Indians, was merely average. Only the man of extraordinary talents could call forth real admiration. Since backwoodsmen and other frontier people valued most their ability to use their rifles, their axes, and their bare fists in subduing the wilderness, the westerner based his ideas of personal worth mainly on the extent to which a man had mastered those techniques.

In his dotage Hall "talked" a good fight, but ample documentary evidence exists to prove that as a younger man his deeds more than justified his words.

Academicians, genealogists and lovers of Texas history will discover a bonanza of fresh material in *Life of Robert Hall.* But most of all, they will meet one of the most colorful, outlandish, and delightful scamps that ever threw his leg over a sadde.

STEPHEN L. HARDIN
Victoria College
October 2, 1992

INTRODUCTORY

I do not claim any literary merit for this book. It was written at a time when I was in very bad health. Both Col. Hall and Mr. Wallace are octogenarians, and age has made them very deaf. In consequence of this fact I labored under a great disadvantage to catch the information that they desired to impart. Often, after asking a dozen times as to some statement, I would still be in doubt as to whether I were recording the facts correctly or not. They hardly hoped that the book would be of sufficient importance to win the attention of the general reading public. I think the old veterans simply troubled themselves for the benefit of relatives, friends, and comrades. I have done the best I could for them, and shall feel myself amply compensated if the little work meets the approval of the old Texans and their descendants.

BRAZOS.

Cotulla, Texas, March 1, 1898.

LIFE OF ROBERT HALL

veteran took a notion that he did not need the services of a metropolitan peace officer. The suit that he wears on gala days and at the gathering of the old veterans is without a doubt the most extraordinary wearing apparel that ever covered and protected the body of an old soldier. He proudly says, 'I made every stitch of it.' The old warrior has been a great hunter, and he has been saving the skins of wild animals for forty years to make this wonderful suit of clothes. The coat is composed of over one hundred different pieces. No two are alike, and each is a piece from the hide of a different wild animal. A piece from the hide of every wild beast and from many reptiles and birds finds a place in the curious and attractive garment. Of course, skins of deer, bears, panthers, wolves and wildcats make up the larger part, but a connoisseur in such matters would readily find pieces from a hundred other animals. The coat is trimmed, or rather ornamented, with the hooves of 315 deer, the claws of forty bears, the tails of innumerable smaller animals and the rattles from hundreds of monster rattlesnakes. His cap is as wonderful as the coat. It is composed of very many pieces of pretty fur, and ornamented with a pair of antelope horns. The old warrior is 6 feet 4 inches high and 85 years of age. He walks with a firm step, carrying his head erect, and when he appears on the streets of San Antonio or at some gathering of veterans wearing this extraordinary suit, he is always the observed of all observers. He wears Indian moccasins of the most fantastic pattern, and sometimes carries a fine sword that he captured from a Mexican officer at the battle of Buena Vista. He fired the first shot in that famous battle. When Gen. Taylor received orders to cross the Rio Grande he looked around among the Texas troops for soldiers—Indian fighters—who were familiar with frontier warfare, and of the men selected to form the vanguard of his army the most conspicuous was Robert Hall, then a young man. Hall was a fearless rider and a daring soldier, always eager for battle. His meritorious conduct in the early skirmishes soon caught the attention of the commander of the army. In the first battle of any consequence young Hall distinguished himself by leading a cavalry charge, and old 'Rough and Ready,' as the soldiers called him, rewarded the young man by making him a confidential scout and spy. The old man's eye kindles with martial fire at the mention of the name of Buena Vista. He thinks it was the greatest battle ever fought on earth.

"'Think of it,' he says, 'We had less than 5000 men, and the Mexican lines stretched as far as the eye could see in every direction. I thought there was no end to them. I was in advance of our picket lines and as the enemy came up I raised my rifle and fired at an advancing column and galloped back to our lines. Gen. Taylor was not on the field at that instant. After the battle we learned that my first shot was not lost on the wind, and for that reason I possess a very fine sword which Gen. Taylor permitted me to keep.'

"The old warrior thinks he has been a hundred times under fire, but he regards the battle of the Salado as the only battle fought in Texas that is worth mentioning.

"It is well known to all students of history that the affair of the Salado was not a skirmish, but the old veteran regards it as ranking with Thermopylae. This occurred in 1842. The Mexicans and Indians, 1500 strong, and commanded by the veteran Gen. Woll, who had learned the art of war under Marshal Soult, were securely posted on a field well selected for military operations, when 200 Texans, under the famous old Paint Caldwell, charged them and started them on a retreat which did not end until they had crossed the Rio Grande. Mr. Hall was wounded in this battle. He has been wounded three times. At the battle of Plum Creek, where Gen. Felix Huston won a great victory over the Comanches, an Indian drove an arrow through Col. Hall's thigh. He kept on his feet until the battle was over, and then calmly asked a friend to pull the arrow from his leg. In this battle the Comanches suffered their final overthrow, and Texas witnessed the end of their long reign of terror.

"Col. Hall as born in South Carolina, and when a mere boy his people moved to Tennessee and settled at Choctaw Bluffs, now Memphis. They built at the mouth of Wolf Creek, as he remembers the name, the first house ever erected by white people where the metropolis of Tennessee now stands. He enlisted with a company of Kentuckians, commanded by Capt. Earl in Harrison's regiment at Natchez, and marched straight to Gen. Houston's army in Texas, joining the patriot warriors a few days after the battle of San Jacinto. Col. Hall more than once stood guard over Santa Anna while the famous dictator was a prisoner in the camp of the victorious Texans. He served during the war, and then enlisted to fight Indians. He was one of the band famous in Texas history who followed and fought the Comanches that had murdered the Taylor family. The battle, which was a desperate affair, occurred on the banks of the Brazos, near where the great stream is joined by the Navasota, now a region of country under the highest state of cultivation and inhabited by the most wealthy and prosperous people in the State. At this battle the old gentleman says he had a close call for his life. He fought three Indians single handed, and making two bite the dust, he conquered the last one by breaking his neck with his fist. From the dead body of this warrior Col. Hall took the bloody scalps of Mrs. Taylor and her children. Col. Hall married a daughter of Col. King, another famous veteran, who escaped the massacre of Fannin's men, and he built the first house in the town of Gonzales, in 1837.

"When the Texas Rangers were organized under the laws of the old Lone Star Republic, Col. Hall and Gen. Henry McCulloch were aspirants for the office of captain of the first company organized, and McCulloch was elected by five votes. That was the first step in his career which led to the command of a great army. Col. Hall seems to regret that particular defeat, and laughingly says, 'I was just as good a soldier as Old Henry, and if I had been elected I might have become a great general.'

"He has been offered $500 for the frontiersman suit that he sometimes wears, but he would not take $10,000 for it. At the last reunion of the veterans, Col. Hall, in this suit, was the most conspicuous figure on the grounds. It occurred at Seguin, and at that time Gov. Ireland and Gen. Burleson were both alive, and they vied with each other in their attention to Col. Hall. 'Big Foot' Wallace, the hero of Mier, who also lives in this vicinity, accompanied Col. Hall to the reunion, where they were made to ride in a carriage, given a seat on the rostrum, and made to listen to the story of their battles, painted in glowing terms by the famous orators in Texas.

"Col. Hall was a great favorite with Gen. Sam Houston, and they were always the warmest of friends. He has the most beautiful hunting horn on the continent. This horn has a strange history. It is covered with beautiful carvings. Sea nymphs, mermaids, ships and dragons of the deep are so delicately intermingled that one could spend hours turning it about and admiring the wonderful work of the artist. It is very long, and at the large end are the words 'El Pirata.' Thereby hangs a tale. Just after the battle of New Orleans, Col. James Long, an officer who had distinguished himself in the great conflict and won the approbation of Gen. Jackson, led a small colony to Texas. He fell into trouble, and after a battle his little army was defeated, and Long was carried to the City of Mexico a prisoner in chains. His wife, who was a niece of the famous Gen. Wilkinson, who figured so prominently as a witness against Aaron Burr, remained in Texas and sought the protection of the pirate Lafitte, who was at that time located on Galveston Island. The buccaneer treated his distinguished guest with every mark of respect, and on one occasion gave a dinner in her honor on board of his flagship. While at the table one of Lafitte's officers showed Mrs. Long a horn, which he said had been taken from the dead body of a pirate. It passed from hand to hand around the table, and every one admired it. Mrs. Long expressed a desire to possess it, and the polite 'terror of the Southern seas' at once handed it to her. Mrs. Long gave the horn to Gen. Sam Houston, and Gen. Houston presented it to Col. Robert Hall for his gallant conduct in battle against the Comanches. Col. Hall is not a poor man. He is pretty well fixed, as the Texans say, but he says, 'If I were out of bread, it would take a million to buy that horn.'

"A short time ago Col. Hall and 'Big Foot' Wallace happened to be in Seguin at the same time. It was no sooner learned that the old heroes were in the city than the boys were hunting for them with a carriage and a band of music. They were found at one of the hotels and the crowd carried Col. Hall out into the street and told him he had to make a speech. 'No,' said the old warrior, straightening himself and apparently shaking two or three decades from his shoulders, 'I can't make a speech; but, boys, if you will play me something quick and devilish I will dance a jig.' The band played his Satanic Majesty's nocturnal revelry and these two old warriors danced on the pavement like boys, and the people of old Seguin hurrahed and told them that they owned the town."

Chapter II.

EARLY LIFE OF ROBERT HALL.

I was born in South Carolina on April 14th, 1814. My father's name was James B. Hall, and my mother's maiden name was Rebecca Gassamary.[*] My grandfather's name was Fanton Hall. He was of Irish descent, and I am pretty certain served in the Revolutionary army.

We lived on the old Charleston road, which was at that time traveled a great deal, in what was then known as the Rocky river district.

There were not many school houses in the country, but we had one old log church, and everybody within twenty miles of it came there every Sunday. I have seen a great many distinguished characters at that old church. I have seen General Jackson and John C. Calhoun. I regard General Jackson as one of the greatest men that ever lived, except Sam Houston.

Our people, in fact every one in the neighborhood, were Hard-Shell Baptist. The world would be better if there were more people of that religion now. Why, I have seen one of the old congregations turn a man out of church because he refused to pay a debt. They used very frequently to turn people out of the church for refusing to keep strangers over night. It was a great church, and I wonder why it did not grow and help us along in this corrupt age of the world.

---

[*] Gassaway [Editor].

From my earliest youth I was very fond of fishing and hunting. Before I was able to handle a gun I could bring down wild game with a bow and arrow with the dexterity of an Indian, and when my people were afraid for me to load an old flint-lock musket, some of the old negroes would load the gun and follow me into the woods. There was an abundance of game at that time, and I generally made that one load count. It was seldom that I ever missed a shot.

The people of South Carolina were very poor. I remember that the proudest and happiest day of my life was when my mother gave me a pair of jeans pants. They had been colored with copperas and the buttons were made of pieces of gourd covered with cloth. Although I was barefooted and had on a flax linen shirt, I would not have traded places with the President of the United States when I put on those pants. There were six children in the family. I think they are all dead, but one sister who is living in Gibson county, Tennessee. I have one daughter living in Blackville, South Carolina. I was very strong and industrious, and before I was grown I had accumulated considerable property. About this time I concluded to sow a crop of wild oats. I engaged in the business with all my might, and the result was that I soon found myself out of money and my face set toward the wild and woolly west. When I left South Carolina there were three hundred Halls, and they could have all been gathered at one spot with the blast of a good horn. I went back there in 1865 and could only find two of the descendants of the once powerful family.

In 1828 game got scarce in South Carolina and we concluded to move to the new District of Tennessee. We settled on the Rutherford fork of the O'Brien,* in Gibson county. My father died in 1833 and was buried in Gibson county, Tennessee.

---

* Probably the Obion River [Editor].

Photo courtesy of Lynn Glenewinkle

Robert Hall wearing his reflector hunting hat

I must have been one of the hardiest and toughest of boys. When I was six or seven years old I frequently hunted rabbits in the snow all day. I was always glad to see the snow, and I don't remember that my feet ever got cold. I would track the rabbits and often catch them without the dogs. I never saw a pair of boots of any kind until I was about sixteen years old. The word sickness conveyed no meaning to my mind, and about the time we moved to Tennessee I was growing up one of the wildest and most consummate young scamps in all America. My recollection of the times and the people causes me to think that the country people were stronger, healthier and happier than they are to-day. It was the boast of my father that the latchstring had hung on the outside of his door for more than half a century. This was not an isolated case. Everybody was hospitable, and it was seldom that we ever heard of a crime. There were few doctors and very little litigation. There was always some old woman in the neighborhood who went to see the sick with a little sack of "herbs." I remember a good story of Gen. Jackson. He was a pretty wild colt in his young days, and he could not make money enough practicing law to pay his board. Finally he was appointed United States Attorney for the District of Tennessee. He left the Carolinas owing his landlord $26, which he promised to pay out of the first money he earned in the West. Time rolled on, but the $26 remained unpaid. The debt was barred by the statute of limitations, but one day the old landlord picked up a paper and read about the great victory at New Orleans. He deliberately walked into his office and wrote, "Settled in full by the battle of New Orleans."

Chapter III.

We raised a fine crop in Tennessee and I got a little money in my pockets and it made a fool of me. I thought that I was bigger, stouter and smarter than my brother and I undertook to thrash him. That turned out to be a game that two could play at, and the first thing I knew I found that I had been taught a pretty good lesson. Brushing the dust from my jeans I ran off and jumped aboard the first flat boat that came floating down the river. The crew was hard set, and they made all sorts of sport of me. The wonder is that they did not drown me, for I am sure they cared very little for human life. I think they would have thrown a tenderfoot overboard at any moment if the act would have raised a laugh. One day they told me the river was rising and they had me to drive a nail in the side of the boat at the water line and watch it. How the pirates did laugh. I soon caught on, however, and only for the grace of God and my good fortune I soon would have been as big a devil as the worst of them. I got off at New Madrid. There were plenty of people living there then who remembered all about the great earthquake. There were great cracks in the earth, and the shores of the river were still covered with miles of drift. The government had a steamboat called the H.M. Shrieve, which the river people were using in trying to open a channel. The Shrieve was rigged for a snag boat, and I enlisted on her and worked about a month. It was a terrible job. The river was a solid mat of logs for miles—looking more like a monster grounded raft than anything else. There came a rise in the river and moved the drift sufficiently that the boats could get through it. One of the first boats to pass was a little steamboat called the Paul Jones. Strangely enough, Mark Twain learned to be a pilot on the Paul Jones under old Horace Bixby, but it could not have been the same boat, for Mr. Twain did not go on the river until late in the fifties. Horace Bixby is living yet. During the war I saw a steamboat named the H.M. Shrieve. I knew it could not have been my old ship. Her bones have mingled with the Mississippi sands long, long ago.

I shipped next on the Hibernia, and while on this boat I saw the notorious John A. Murrel. We were going through a bayou down near New Orleans, and had great difficulty during the night in keeping the boat in the channel. There was considerable gambling in the cabin and some big games. It had been hinted that there was a desperate character on the boat, but it never occurred to the passengers that he was the celebrated John A. Murrel. Murrel had a bunch of stateroom keys, and had been plundering the passenger's baggage during the night. Just at daylight a traveler caught the robber in his room. Fortunately for Murrel, just at that instant the boat ran against the shore, and he tore loose from the grasp of the passenger and sprang over the guard into the canebrake. He dropped a bunch of three hundred keys. The shout was raised, "There goes John A. Murrel!" and several shots were fired at him, but as we afterwards learned he escaped unharmed.

Chapter IV.

HIS CAREER AS A FLATBOATMAN—HE TAMES A DESPERADO.

Next year I went up to Tennessee and built a flat boat and launched her on the South Fork of the O'Brien. I freighted her with 1500 bushels of corn, and hired a pilot to steer me into the Mississippi. We floated down the Coldwater, the shores of which presented many curiosities of flora and fauna. We found some of the largest skeletons here I ever saw. This region must at sometime have been inhabited by a race of giants. We saw human heads twice as large as the head of an ordinary man, while the teeth in the jaws were like the teeth of some colossal animal. We camped at one place where evidently a great battle had been fought. Acres and acres of the country were covered with bleaching bones—and such bones! There were thigh and arm bones that made us think of Og-Gog and Magog. The whole country was then a wilderness. Only here and there we met a squatter or a hunter. There was a little settlement on the Yazoo called Manchester, now Yazoo City. There I sold my cargo and craft and instantly proceeded to sow a crop of wild oats, but I had learned a little sense by this time, and did not go too far. Here I had a close call for my life: A desperado by the name of Phelps who had been engaged in robbing the mail in Arkansas turned up in Chula and proclaimed himself a cross between a cyclone and a wildcat. He claimed the town on the first day of arrival and began to look around for a suitable location for a private graveyard. "A bowie knife," he said, "was his looking glass, and a pistol shot was soothing music to his soul." He had several hundred dollars in money, and when he asked people to drink with him he invariably pushed back the change. He said that he could not sleep until he had had a fight. It became evident that the gentleman from Arkansas intended to shed blood before he retired, and after talking the matter over the boys concluded that I was the man to tame him. He was a powerful man, but I tackled him and disarmed him. In the affair a pistol shot passed close to may head. I arrested him and took him to Hines to jail. After I had turned the keys on him two of his friends attacked me. They were both giants in strength. It was the most desperate and dangerous battle I had ever fought. I barely managed to prevent them from killing me. My strength alone saved me. I had to fight one of these men again. Oliver challenged me and we selected our seconds and went out a mile from town. We fought a fist fight and I whipped him in two minutes. There were a great many people present and it was regarded as a most remarkable affair.

The next year I was employed by a very wealthy planter named Charles McGee to go to Memphis to buy a cargo of corn. By this time I had got to be a pretty good pilot myself, and I purchased a good flat boat and freighted her with 2000 bushels of corn and slipped her cables and set out once more for the Yazoo. This voyage was uneventful, and I pleased Mr. McGee so well that he gave me a thousand dollars a year to oversee his plantation. About this time we heard of the war in Texas, and I became restless to join Gen. Sam Houston's army.

Chapter V.

REMINISCENCES OF DAVY CROCKETT—WHIPS A GIANT.

The first vote I ever cast was for old Davy Crockett. We lived in the same neighborhood in Tennessee. Crockett was a candidate for Congress against Col. Huntsman. Crockett never missed a gathering of any kind. He was always present at every frolic, log rolling, or house raising. He was certainly one of the most popular men that ever lived. He had said that if Huntsman beat him that his opponent might go to h—l and that he would go to Texas. Col. Crockett happened to meet me in McLemoreville on the day of the election, and he said, "Hello, Bob, have you voted?" I had not thought of it, as I was only eighteen years old, but some old veteran marched me to the polls and I voted. Of course it was wrong, but I have never regretted it. I never look at the Alamo and think of the brave old warrior's cruel death, without wishing that I had possessed a thousand votes to cast for him that day.

About this time I had a fight which was the talk of the whole State for a long time. There had been bitter enmity between the settlers on either side of a little creek called Rutherford's fork of the O'Brien, in Gibson county, Tennessee. The people on one side of the creek hated the people on the other side with all the bitterness of wild Indians. I lived on the west side of the creek, and on the east side of the creek lived a man by the name of Louis Witherbry, who was regarded as one of the most perfect specimens of physical manhood in the west. He weighed 200 pounds, and there was not an ounce of surplus flesh on him. Besides all this he was a trained athlete and frequently boasted that he did not believe there was a man on earth who could hit him with a sledge hammer. He had frequently declared that he could whip me with one hand tied behind him. I had never been whipped, thrown down, or defeated in a running match. I knew I was a strong man, but I was never quarrelsome. My friends were anxious for me to meet this giant and tame him, for he was a great fellow to brag and blow his own horn. Finally the opportunity came. There was a horse race, and I went, knowing very well that I would have to fight before the day ended. The giant's brother began the fight. He cursed me and I knocked him down. Then the big bully told me to strip myself and we would have a fair fight. The people were all greatly interested in the battle, and they formed a ring and appointed good men to see fair play. We clinched and fell early in the fight. I instantly saw that I was the strongest man, and I determined never to let him up. He bit me badly on the lip, but I managed to get my arms around his body and I held him so that he could not move. I could not release my arms to strike him, and concluding that all strategy was fair in war, I used my teeth. The doctors said that I bit nine pieces out of his back. He was yelling all the time like a Comanche in the fire, but I would not let him up until he shouted "'nough." Then the boys made a hero of me. They carried me on their shoulders all over the grounds, and the ladies clapped their hands and hurrahed for the "eighteen year old boy who had whipped the big bully."

Chapter VI.

HUNTING IN ARKANSAS.

My brother heard that game was very abundant in Arkansas, and he came back to Tennessee with glowing accounts of the new country, and easily persuaded me that we could soon make a fortune trapping and trading with the Indians in the Saline river region. The country was not misrepresented as far as game was concerned. Deer would not exactly come into camp and lick salt out of your hand, but they would come to the salt-licks in droves, and the crack of the rifle did not seem to disturb them. We helped to move the Choctaw Indians to their reservation, where they still live. They were brought up White river on little boats to a place called Rockrun, not far from Grand Prairie. I am not sure, but I think Gen. Scott was there for a few days. Here we experienced something that presented more horrors than war or anything else I have ever witnessed. The Indians had hardly gone into camp before Asiatic cholera broke out among them. Bucks, squaws and children died like sheep with the rot. It was terrible to witness their sufferings. They attributed everything to the magic and deviltry of the white man, and few of them could be induced to take any medicine. They did not want to go to the reservation, and I expect many of them wandered off and died in the woods. There was a tall army officer who had great influence with them. He was an officer of high rank, and I am inclined to think he was no other than Gen. Scott. I was with Gen. Taylor in Mexico and never saw Gen. Scott in my life, unless I saw him at that time. We finally got the Indians in army wagons and started on the march.

Though they were dying every few hours, the movement seemed to have abated the epidemic. After a few days, to our utmost delight, there were only a few sick people in camp. A great many American soldiers and teamsters died, but I escaped the disease.

There were no towns in the country but Little Rock and a few houses at Hot Springs. We met an old trapper from Ohio by the name of Jennings. He had served in Harrison's campaigns against the Indians. He was at the battle of Tippecanoe, where he said he had a good look at the dead body of Tecumseh.* He was in the little fort defended by the gallant Major Crogham. He only knew one story, and this he used to tell at the camp fire every night. He said that Major Crogham developed into a great drunkard, and that Gen. Jackson was frequently asked to dismiss him from the army. Finally some officer approached Old Hickory on the subject with great earnestness, saying that Crogham was drunk all the time and that he was a disgrace to the army and ought to be retired. Old Hickory in his impatience snorted out: "By the eternal gods, Crogham held his fort against the British and the Indians and he has got a right to be drunk all his life, and the Government has got to pay for the whisky." This old curiosity went with us down on the Saline, and built us a house out of pine bark, and it was a good house, too. It would turn water like a shingle roof. This was the first house ever built on the Saline river. I am inclined to think that we were located not very far from where the battle of Jenkins' Ferry was fought during the Civil War. The old man Jennings helped to whip the Indians near where the city of Cincinnati now is. After the battle the soldiers agreed

---

* While the trapper reports he saw the dead body of Tecumseh at the battle of Tippecanoe, Tecumseh was not killed until 5 October 1813 during the war of 1812 [Editor].

to meet there on the 50th anniversary of the conflict. The old pioneer kept that idea in his head during all his wanderings for half a century, and when the fifty years had passed he put on his best buckskin suit and started for the Paris of America. He reached there all right and had sense enough to go to the Enquirer office and tell his story. The editor wrote him up and they found one man who had been in the battle near the city fifty years before. This man's name was Ellis. He lived in Cincinnati. The town loaded old man Jennings with presents and he had wonderful stories to tell when he came back to Little Rock.

We killed game enough on the Saline during the winter to have supplied a city, and in the spring we returned to old Tennessee with a fine lot of furs. Here I once more met Col. Davy Crockett. He was at a log rolling. It was a grand affair. The boys selected captains and divided forces. Crockett took his liquor out of a gourd. Right then he was talking a great deal about going to Texas. The boys worked like tigers, and, as the jug was very handy, long before sundown they were ready for almost any affair that promised fun and frolic. There was an old poplar log on the field that had been fired. No hundred men could have moved it, but the captains insisted that an attempt should be made to get it out of the way. It had been raining a little, and the log was as black and sticky as jet. Col. Crockett was the first man to tackle it, and in two minutes he was blacker than midnight in her zenith. Everybody laughed at him, and he swore he would change the color of every man on the ground. He did it, and then he sent a negro for a fiddle, and he played a tune that sometimes soothes my old tired brain even to this day. That was the last big frolic that grand old Davy Crockett ever had in the land he loved so well.

No event ever created such a sensation or so much talk as what was known as the "star falling night." People did not know what to make of the strange phenomenon. They expected it to be repeated, and nearly every one was sure that the end of the world was not far distant. Prophets sprang up in every neighborhood and spread the most unbounded alarm among the people. Many people sat up during the succeeding nights until they were worn out. Neighbors gathered at the house of some minister and spent the night on their knees. Many ludicrous things happened. A white man and a negro were building a flat boat seven miles from home. When the heavens became illuminated with the shooting flames they dropped their tools and started on a dead run for home. One would have supposed that under the influence of fright they would have run themselves to death. Strangely enough, they both reached the house alive. The sentiment that makes the story worth printing is found in the fact that the man who ran seven miles from shooting meteors lived to be elected to Congress.

side-wheeler named George Washington, bound for Red river. It was a slow boat and we were a long time reaching our destination. We went ashore at an old town called Nacitosh. From there we marched to Natchitoches, and from there to San Augustine. There we met Gen. Sam Houston, suffering from the wound he had received at San Jacinto. He did all he could to encourage us, saying: "There is plenty of fine land in Texas and I hope to see you all have good homes." We were not well prepared for the hard march that was in front of us. We were without money or army supplies. We set out on foot to join the army, then in camp on the La Vaca. It was a pretty hard march. We crossed the Brazos at Old Washington. Here we camped and rested several days. The people of the town treated us with extraordinary hospitality, supplying our camp with the best that they had. There was not much town there. There was an abundance of wild game; we were hardly ever out of sight of deer. We moved next in the direction of Columbus on the Colorado. There was only one house there, and no one lived in that. A few days afterwards we reached the Texas army, which was at that time commanded by Albert Sidney Johnston. It was called "Camp Johnston." The army was at that time about 2000 strong, but very poorly equipped, and with scarcely any commissary supplies. We were there nearly four months, and during all that time I never saw a piece of bread. We lived entirely on beef, but the soldiers were in good spirits until something like dysentery broke out and a great many died. I think at least 300 brave fellows were wrapped in their blankets and laid away in the earth in that camp. I was very near death myself in this camp, but an old veteran named Jack Bray waited on me and saved my life. I never knew what became of him. While in this camp Karnes and Teal came to us. They had been captured by the Mexicans and imprisoned at Matamoras. Their friends had long mourned them as dead; no one expected to see either of them alive. One day they straggled into camp nearly naked and half famished. They had broke jail at Matamoras and traveled several hundred miles. The gunners at once ran out the batteries and fired many rounds of welcome, while the soldiers carried the poor fellows about the camp on their shoulders. Teal was afterward appointed commander of the army, but he was assassinated in his tent. The affair was alway a mystery, as it was not known that the brave man had an enemy on earth.

About this time I made the acquaintance of one of the greatest and most unassuming patriots that ever shouldered a musket in the cause of Texas. His name was Dimmitt. He was a Kentuckian and came to Texas many years before the revolution. He married a Spanish wife and settled at Dimmitt's Point. He had built a fine house and was pretty well off. He was always ready to divide any thing and every thing he had with us. He was a man of no mean ability and might easily have assumed high rank with the distinguished patriots who established the country, but he preferred to act with those who handled muskets. He had a large herd of fat cattle, and he told the commander of the army to "slay and eat." Texans have honored him by naming a county after him.

In the fall of 1836 we were all pretty well satisfied that there would be no more fighting, and we were anxious to get discharged from the army. We had been living on beef alone for so long that the patriotism had begun to die out of us, and the best of us would have traded our interest in the fortune of the Lone Star Republic for a good big skillet of cornbread. I was awful weak and getting awful sick of the inactivity and hardships of army life. I was well acquainted with Dr. Woods and I went to him several times to get a discharge, which he invariably refused to grant. I had a very fine pair of saddle pockets which Dr. Woods always wanted. One day when I was feeling worse than usual I walked into his tent and threw these saddle bags at his feet and politely asked him for a discharge from the army. He wrote it out very quick and told me to "clear out." I did not stand on the order of going. I started at once for Columbia, which was then the capital of the Republic. I had a little money and I was thinking all the time of the good things—such as corn bread—that I would buy when I got to town. On the road I suddenly came upon an old negro woman who was churning. I scented the buttermilk afar off, and never in my life did I taste anything as sweet as that buttermilk. I drank enough of it to kill an ordinary man, and it smelled sweeter than attar of roses and tasted more glorious than liquor of the peach intermingled with honey of the wild bee.

When I got to Columbia, Congress was in session and nearly all the noted men of the Republic were in town. Everybody was in good spirits. We realized that we were in a good country and that there was land enough to make us all rich. We had demonstrated on the field of San Jacinto that the Republic was able to protect itself. Santa Anna was still a prisoner at the capital, and he was constantly assuring the President and his cabinet that there would never be any more war between Mexico and Texas. I went to see him while I was in Columbia, and since the history of Texas could not be written without mentioning his name, I will present him to my friends as I remember him.

Chapter VIII.

GENERAL SANTA ANNA.

I had opportunities for knowing the man better than other Americans. I saw a great deal of him while he was a prisoner in our camp, after the battle of San Jacinto, and I also saw him upon several occasions while he was in command of his army during the Mexican war. The conduct of the Texans in sparing the life of the Butcher of the Alamo has been regarded as an incredible act of clemency. The fact is that Santa Anna deserved death; but he was the head of the Mexican government, and men who reasoned wiser than others hoped that a permanent peace might be made with him and the war forever ended. Gen. Houston was one of the greatest of men, and the very first words his distinguished prisoner uttered gave the old commander a key to the character of the man whose whole career had been written in innocent blood. He begged for a few grains of opium to sustain him, and no sooner were his nerves steady than he began to flatter the man who held over him the power of life and death. The battle of San Jacinto demonstrated two traits in the character of Santa Anna. One was that he was no general, and the other was that he was a coward. A few days before the great battle Santa Anna summoned several of his generals to his tent and informed them that the war was over. "The Texans," he said, "had been defeated in every battle, and Gen. Houston with the shattered remnant of the army was flying towards the United States." Santa Anna had just received dispatches from the City of Mexico informing him that he had been elevated to supreme power, and he wanted to leave Gen. Filisola in command and return at once to the seat of government. Old soldiers who had fought the Texans in other campaigns dared to differ with the Dictator. They told him that another great battle would have to be fought and a victory won over one of the greatest generals and the most stubborn troops of modern times before Mexico could claim Texas. Santa Anna, governed by the advice of subordinate generals, finally concluded to remain in command of the column of his army that was marching towards the capital.

This is exactly what Gen. Houston hoped for. The Mexicans outnumbered him two to one, but on one side there was genius and courage, and on the other the treachery of the Alamo and the massacre of Fannin's men. Not one of those brilliant military maneuvers which originated in the brain of that master of the art of war while he was crushing the Austrians in Italy is more worthy of the admiration of the student of history than the plan of that short campaign which drew the self-styled Napoleon of the West into a network of bayous and marshes, from which his cannon and musketry were powerless to extricate him.

The battle itself was a master stroke. It was genius seizing the opportune moment. A charge, a hurrah; five minutes of hell or glory—as you please—and a new nation was born.

It is said that Santa Anna and many of his officers were taking a nap in their tents when the battle commenced. No general of any ability would have gone to sleep in daylight within sight of an enemy's camp. Certainly not after he had been informed that the enemy were eager for battle.

Santa Anna had seen many battles. He knew defeat when he saw it, and he no sooner reached the door of his tent than he realized that all was lost. Like all other tyrants, the first thing he thought of was his own personal safety. His own horse had been shot. Col. Juan Bringas dismounted and gave the terrified general his own magnificent stallion. He never made any attempt to rally the troops, but, driving the steel into the flanks of the noble animal, he rode at full speed from the battle field. Reaching Vinces bridge, which he had crossed the day previous, he was surprised to find that it had been destroyed. He did not hesitate, but plunged into the stream at once. The horse perished, but the general managed to reach the opposite shore.

The next morning he was captured and brought into the camp of the Texas patriots. He had changed his uniform with a private soldier, and as a consequence the three soldiers who brought the trembling wretch into camp were ignorant of their prisoner's high rank until the Mexicans began to salute him as "El Presidente." Santa Anna at once asked to be carried into the presence of Gen. Houston. After swallowing a little opium he talked very boldly.

"I am General Antonio Lopez de Santa Anna, and I claim to be your prisoner of war. The man who has conquered the Napoleon of the West in a pitched battle is born to no common destiny, and, general, it devolves upon you to be generous to the vanquished."

Gen. Houston replied: "You ought to have thought of that at the Alamo."

The commander was suffering great pain from the wound that he had received in battle, and the conversation did not last long. Houston knew the feeling in his army against Santa Anna, and he took the precaution not only to have him well guarded, but he summoned the most influential officers and many privates and advised them to treat the wretched man as a prisoner of war. It is doubtful whether any other man on earth could have prevented the Texans from shooting the Butcher of the Alamo on the spot. Nine men out of ten believed that he deserved death, and it is one of the miracles of history that he escaped with his life.

In this affair two things will survive and ever be recorded and remembered to the credit of the Texans. One was their

Chapter IX.

COURTSHIP, COURAGE, MARRIAGE, AND FIRE HUNTING.

After I had rested awhile I started back to Mississippi, but when I reached Montgomery county I fell in love with the country and concluded to settle there. I rode a little Spanish mule from the capital to Montgomery county. A discharged soldier by the name of Smith, who was dead broke, got me to carry his blankets and his other shirt. He was a good fellow and full of life, and I enjoyed his company very much.

The prairies were covered with wild cattle, and Smith thought it great fun to swing his hat over his head and yell like a Comanche, and make the cattle stampede. One day we suddenly came close to an old Texas steer. Smith sprang at him, hat in hand. The steer was not of the running kind; he was full of fight, and he lunged at my comrade, looking more vicious than a grizzly bear, and ten times more dangerous than an American lion. Smith had been in many battles, but this was the first time he ever showed the color of the back of his coat to an enemy. He actually outran the steer, and when I caught up with him he calmly remarked: "Here I have been carrying a fortune in my legs all my life, and never knew it."

During the summer of 1837 I made a fine crop in Montgomery county, on the plantation of a man by the name of Clark. In the meantime I sent to Nacatosh and got my trunk—something that I never expected to see. I had several suits of clothes, and when I dressed up the people looked at me in wonder and astonishment.

About this time I heard of Col. John G. King, who had three of the prettiest girls in Texas. Col. King had settled near Gonzales several years before and improved a fine plantation. He came to Texas with the famous McGee expedition, and was present at the terrible battle of Medina. When Santa Anna invaded Texas, Col. King moved his family to Eastern Texas, but his son, William P. King, joined Travis, and fell at the Alamo. Those who knew this young man say that he was one of the loveliest characters that Texas ever produced. Col. King wanted to go to the Alamo himself, but his son influenced him to take care of the family, saying that "he only wished he had more than one life to give to his country." He died fighting by the side of the brave Crockett.

I dressed myself in my best suit and rode over to Col. King's house, where my heart was at once captured by the beauty of Polly King. The old colonel was absent at the time. He had take a small force and gone to his plantation near Gonzales, where he lived in a fort, and made a crop. He afterwards told me that the worst scare he ever got in his life occurred while he was in that little fort. A herd of frightened buffalo came stampeding through the brush, and some one shouted that they were pack mules. The camp was in an uproar for a few minutes, and the shots that were fired brought down something good to eat instead of Indians and mule meat. The colonel always enjoyed telling this story. He said that it illustrated that the bravest of men became partially blind under excitement and in the face of great danger.

By the time the old man got back, Polly and I were engaged. All the family liked me. A rival by the name of John McGuffin met the old colonel on his road home, and told him that I was a bad man and that I had a wife in the States. He treated me very coolly. I knew there was something wrong, but, feeling conscious of my integrity and the purity of my motives, I concluded to be patient, and hoped to win the old man's approbation by brave, upright, honorable conduct.

An opportunity soon presented itself for me to show the fine old gentleman that I had a heart of gold and the courage of a dozen lions. The Indians made a raid into the settlement, and killed Mrs. Taylor and her little girl, at Fanthorp's, on Grimes prairie. The settlers flew to arms, and Col. King was elected to lead the expedition against the Indians. I was, of course, one of the first volunteers. My soul was in arms and eager for the fray. I wanted Col. King to see me in battle, and I felt pretty sure that if I survived the action that he would give me his daughter. I have described the pursuit in one of the first chapters of this book. After it was all over, Col. King called me to him and simply said: "A brave man never lies. Tell me the truth. Have you got a family back in the States?"

I replied: "Colonel, I was never married in my life, nor did I ever love another girl but your daughter. If you will give her to me I will do everything in my power to make her a good husband."

"Give me your hand, my brave boy," he said. "I believe you will do it."

I was the happiest man in the world. We were married on the 20th of June, 1837. We lived together forty-five years, and thirteen children were born to us. We were always happy together and never happy out of each other's sight. In our old age we did more courting than we did under the swinging moss on the old plantation when we were young and Polly's voice was full of sweeter notes than the mocking birds in the trees.

Col. King was very anxious about his landed possessions at Gonzales, and he invited me to take a trip with him to that country. We camped one night at Groce's, on the Brazos, where Gen. Houston's army had camped for several weeks not long before the battle of San Jacinto. The town of Gonzales had been almost entirely destroyed; there was only one little house remaining. I looked into an old corn crib, and there laid a dead man. He had been killed with arrows. We buried the body. Col. King's crop had not been disturbed, and we calculated that there was corn enough on the plantation to last us for another year.

We started on our return journey, and fell in with French Smith, who was at that time a noted man in Texas. It was said of him that he was the greatest scholar that ever crossed the Sabine. He was a polished orator and a brave soldier, but no influence that could be brought to bear upon him could restrain his intemperance. He might easily have held any position within the gift of the people, but he knew his failing and he would never accept any office. He traveled with us back home.

Just after we crossed Peach creek we struck a fresh Indian trail where at least a hundred warriors had passed. They evidently prepared an ambush for us. We were close enough to them to smell them, but we turned and rode in a different direction.

Col. King thought he was a great runner. He used to say that he did not believe there was an Indian on the plains that could catch him. While we were camped on the Brazos we concluded to take a bath. The old colonel got to looking at my muscles, and he bantered me for a race. French Smith staked off the track and agreed to judge the race. We ran 50 yards, and the judge said that when we came out there was just light between us. The old gentleman was then about 45 years old. It required all the strength and exertion I could put forth to beat him.

After we got home a man asked me to help him move his family up on Grimes prairie. As we were passing along the road I saw a black bear seated on his haunches not far away. I got out of the wagon without saying a word and unhitched one of the horses and mounted him without taking the harness off. Then, swinging my hat over my head, and yelling like an Indian, I rode at a full gallop right at bruin. That was the worst scared bear I ever saw. He did not run more than 300 yards before he ran up a tree. The women and children could not see the bear, as it was in a ravine. They could see me on the harnessed horse, with chains rattling, my hat in the air, and yelling like a Comanche warrior. What on earth did it all mean? They at once jumped to the conclusion that I was crazy, and the women and children sprang out of the wagons and began to run after me, screaming with all their might. When they reached me I had already treed the bear. John Landrum brought a gun and we killed the bear. He was very fat and made fine steak—a thing we particularly needed just at that time.

While on this trip I had rather a strange hunting experience. There were plenty of deer in the country, and I concluded to have a fire hunt. I manufactured a fire lamp and armed myself with an old smooth-bore flint-lock musket that carried forty buckshot. I went out after dark and had no trouble in finding the big game. There seemed to be several of them, and I maneuvered around shining their eyes until I got sight on the biggest pair I ever saw in all my life. Taking deliberate aim, I pulled the trigger, and I am not clear as to the occurrence of this world for the next few moments. It first occurred to me that a steamboat boiler has bursted, and then after my mind had cleared a little I concluded that a cyclone had passed over that particular portion of Texas. I was lying on the ground, and the old musket was still quivering. I think it was trying to get up and kick me again. I struck it a blow with a club to keep it quiet, and about that time I heard something else struggling and possibly trying to get out of the way of the young cannon. I was lying some ten or twelve steps from where I was standing when I pulled the trigger, and several trees were bent and twisted between me and my original position. By a superhuman effort I managed to raise up and feel of myself. I was very much gratified to find that I was all there, but I was afraid that the musket was not satisfied, for it seemed to me that I could hear it cocking itself and sharpening its flint. I got on my feet and started to run away, and in doing so I fell down over one of the biggest old bucks that was ever killed in Texas. Something struck me on the leg, and, fearing that the old musket was after me again, I started to run and fell over another deer.

By this time I was thoroughly alarmed. I had no idea what I had not killed. It was only a short distance to the house, and I feared that some of the shot might have gone on over the hill and killed some of my stock, or perhaps my wife and children. Thoroughly alarmed, I crawled cautiously back to where the old gun was lying. It looked innocent enough, but I was afraid of it. I got around on the safe side of it and took it by the muzzle and held the butt end away from me until I took off my suspenders. Then I tied the terrible thing hard and fast to a tree, and went home and told the folks proudly that I had killed two old bucks at one shot. The wonder is that I did not kill more.

Chapter X.

In the fall of 1837 I had more corn than I needed, and I concluded to take a hundred bushels to Houston. We had no idea what Houston was like, but we needed some groceries, and we thought maybe we could trade the corn for such things as we needed. Col. King had some idea about the roads, and he volunteered to accompany me. We hitched six yoke of cattle to a big wagon, loaded in the corn, and pulled out. At the crossing of Buffalo bayou there was no bridge, but we made a sort of brush pontoon and crossed without any difficulty. To our utter astonishment we found that the city of Houston consisted of three houses. We were afraid that our trip was for nothing, but the old colonel found a man who wanted the corn, and he gave me a hundred dollars in gold for it. There was not a store in the place, but one of the Sheppards (Chauncy's father, I think) owned a little store up in Montgomery county, and there I bought a few groceries.

While in Houston we heard a very strange story. The steamboat Yellow Stone had been sunk somewhere near the mouth of the Brazos, and Captain Earl, whose name has been mentioned in this book, undertook to float her for a certain sum of money. The Texans were very much attached to the Yellow Stone. She had brought the Twin Sisters and lots of recruits to the old patriot army. Upon one occasion she had run through Santa Anna's army. Her engines and pilot house were protected by cotton bales. The Mexicans fired hundreds of musket shots at her, and hundreds of cannon balls, but she sailed serenely along with her nose up and the Lone Star flag floating proudly from her jack staff.

At one point, where the channel came close to the shore, a cavalry officer ordered some vaqueros to throw their lariats over the chimneys. A few of the dare-devils succeeded in accomplishing their design, and the result can be better imagined than described. They were doubtless anxious to get some one to help them turn her loose.

In Houston we heard that Captain Earl had succeeded in raising the boat. No sooner done than he raised steam and sailed away for the waters of the Mississippi, and we never heard of him or the Yellow Stone afterwards. Texas would like to have her bones. She was to us what the Constitution was to the old sea dogs of the old wars, the Victory to the English, and La Belle Poole to the French.

Later in the fall we became pretty certain that Mexico would not send another army against us, and we all moved back to Gonzales. Col. King's plantation was about nine miles from Gonzales, on the north side of the Guadalupe, in the direction of Seguin. Here we built a little log fort and prepared to settle down for life.

In 1838 we made a fine crop. A fine old Texan named Mark Dikes lived with us that year. He was a nice old gentleman. We never knew what became of him. There were no mills in the country, but Col. King and I took two small steel mills out with us to grind corn.

In the fall of '38 fifty of us clubbed together and bought half a league of land from old Joe Martin and laid off the town of Seguin. I was one of the chain carriers. The deer were so plentiful that they would hardly get out of our way. They acted as if they were not at all afraid of us. One day an old doe came smelling around where I was carrying the chain, and I picked up a rock and threw it at her, breaking her leg. One would have

Photo courtesy of Lawrence T. Jones III

Robert Hall, Hunter

Photo courtesy of Dallas Historical Society Collections

Screen actor Gary Cooper tries on Robert Hall's coat as Texas historian
Herbert Gambrell looks on.

thought she would have run off after that, but she did not. She limped around camp for several months, and the boys called her "Hall's old doe."

Here we endured some very remarkable hardships. My wife finally got down to one dress. This hurt me very badly. She patiently bore her distress, however, and patched this one dress until it would have been impossible to distinguish the original material. One day I heard of a little store about a hundred miles away, and that night I told Polly I intended to go to it and get her some dresses. She began to cry and declared I should not go; but I told her I had a good horse and a good gun, and that I was going to get her a dress. The Indians were awfully bad that fall, but I could not bear to see my wife in rags. The store was at a place called Texana, on the Navidad. I started early in the morning and rode day and night. I never saw a white face or built a fire. I made the trip in a little more than two days. Polly was surprised to see me so soon. I bought her two dresses, as many groceries as I could pack, and many other little things to please a woman's heart.

Chapter XI.

PURSUIT OF THE COMANCHES, WHO HAD CAPTURED TWO GIRLS.

A good many families were settling on the frontier, and it became necessary to organize a military company for the protection of the people. We could only raise twenty-nine men, and we elected old Paint Caldwell, a noted Indian fighter, captain, and Chas. Lockhart was made first lieutenant, and I served as second lieutenant. Old Paint, as they called him, was a curiosity. The boys called him Old Paint from the fact that he had white spots on his breast like a paint horse.

The Comanches made a raid into the settlement, and they happened upon a lot of young folks who were gathering pecans in the bottoms of the Guadalupe. They captured one young lady by the name of Lockhart and one named Miss Putnam, and five children. This was on Sunday evening. Monday our company got together and went to a noted Indian crossing on the Guadalupe, at what was known as the Capotes. We placed sentinels at the ford, but we saw no Indians. We struck the trail at the crossing of the old San Antonio road on the Santa Clara. The trail passed right through where the town of Marion now stands, and on the head of the Guadalupe. I was in advance, and when I got on a ridge I saw the Indian camp. I think there must have been at least a thousand warriors. I reported to the captain. It was agreed to leave it to the rank and file whether we should attack the enemy at once or not. The order was given for all who were in favor of advancing to step to the front. Just one-half of the men were in favor of battle. Old Paint had the casting vote, and he favored a retreat. At that time many of us were very mad at him, but years of experience in Indian warfare has taught me that he was right. The Indians outnumbered us fifty to one, and if we had charged them not a soul would have been left to tell the story of the slaughter. We retired back to the Comal. The Indian signs were thick and looked fresh. We were out of provisions, and Capt. Caldwell asked me if I would risk trying to kill some game. I went down the Comal to a little prairie where I saw six buffalo standing out in the prairie as if they were asleep. Their heads were all one way. I advanced until I got right in front of their heads. Just as I was about ready to shoot I saw two of our men creeping on the same herd. I selected a fat cow and aimed well. At the crack of the gun the blood spurted from the cow's side and she reeled away from the herd. I knew she would not go far, and I went back to camp and asked Capt. Caldwell for fifteen men. I had heard a shot after I left and I was afraid the Indians had killed the two other men that I had seen. Fifteen men, well armed, mounted their horses and galloped back with me to where I had shot the cow. We had no difficulty in finding the dead animal, and when we transported the fat carcass to camp there was great rejoicing. Nearly the whole camp sat up around the fires, roasting and eating buffalo meat, all night.

We returned home and disbanded. It was a matter of great regret with the frontier settlers that we were not strong enough to fight the red devils who held the two young ladies and several children captives.

Chapter XII.

INDIAN WARS—STRANGE STORY OF A CAPTURED GIRL.

During these unhappy times the Indians raided the frontier settlements nearly every month. They always came down from the mountains in the light of the moon. Upon one occasion they were so bold as to attack the town of Seguin. I think that they only intended to steal horses. They came near the town in the night, and cautiously walked into the streets, "quacking" like ducks. This gave them away, for there was not a duck in the town. The alarm that "there were Indians in town" was instantly raised, and every male citizen flew to arms and rushed upon the red devils from every side. The Indians were seized with panic and fled to the mountains, leaving their arms and accoutrements stacked and piled under some trees just outside of the town.

Upon one occasion a party of Indians came down near Col. King's place and built a corral. Col. Clemens and Col. King owned some very fine horses. The Indians got them all and got a pretty good start before we discovered the theft. We followed the trail and came upon two of the Indians lying asleep under a tree. There were four of us, and we charged them at once. I made a bad shot and barely grazed my Indian's head. Col. Clemens shot his Indian as he ran away and killed him dead. I followed my Indian, loading my gun as I galloped after him. He would have gotten away from me if I had not had an old dog that kept close to his heels. I shot at him several times. The red devil would sometimes look back at me and shout, "Knockmah!" I do not know what he meant, but I think he was begging me not to kill him. He was entirely naked, and my last shot wounded him pretty badly. The blood streamed from his side, and that set my old dog wild. At last the dog caught him, and he said "knockmah" for the last time. The band had divided, and another party captured the remainder of our horses.

The next day I raised a company and followed the Blanco to the Twin Sisters. We could see Indian signals in every direction, but they never offered to give us battle. As we returned home we killed a Spanish cow. We found eight of our men on this trip that the Indians had killed some days previous. They were surveyors, and it looked as if they had built a fire and gone to sleep in camp without placing out any guards. They were all shot in the head. One man by the name of Wallace, who was known to have been with the party, was never found. It is possible that he was wounded and ran off in the woods and perished.

When the Indians captured the party of girls that were gathering pecans, they carried off one little baby. Years afterwards the Indians told the traders that the child was adopted by a squaw. They said that the squaw died and they killed the child and buried it with its adopted mother. A man named Shinalt bought a twelve-year-old white girl from the Indians. He afterwards came on a visit with his family down on the Guadalupe. Old settlers soon saw the girl, and they declared that she must be the baby that was stolen by the Indians years before. They based their belief on the young girl's striking resemblance to the Putnam family. The Putnam people came to see her, and they said that the matter could be easily settled. The baby, they said, had a great scar on her hip. The girl no sooner heard this than she burst into tears. "I have the scar," she said. Her people took her home. The other girls were all rescued in the course of time save one. A girl named Putnam married an Indian warrior, and no amount of persuasion could

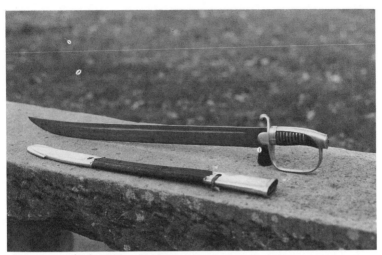

Photo courtesy of Deborah Bloyce Hardin

Sword taken by Robert Hall during the Mexican War

ever induce her to return to civilization. Her descendants are still well known among the Indians.

One day Col. King was hauling a load of rock. He had gotten nearly home when he noticed that the tire had come off of one of his wheels. He unhitched one of his horses and went back to look for it. About the time he found the tire he found a Tonkaway Indian in full war paint. The old gentleman was unarmed, and he wheeled his horse and fled for his life. He was riding a splendid horse and soon distanced his pursuer. The Indian kept calling out to him in Spanish that he wanted a friendly talk. The colonel told him to lay down his bow and arrows and advance. The Indian did so. He said that his tribe had just fought a great battle with the Mexicans on the Nueces, and that they had been defeated. He said that they wanted to make a treaty of peace with the Texans. This was something that the people of Texas were very anxious to do. Col. King invited the Indian to his house, and he sent me after Capt. Caldwell. The Indian summoned other noted Indians of the

Chapter XIII.

LIPANS EAT A COMANCHE.

The Lipans were very strong at this time. It was said that they could put 500 warriors in the field any day. There had been rumors that this powerful tribe wanted to make peace with us, but we did not believe it. One day I looked from the door of my house and saw not less than a thousand mounted warriors not a mile away. They were mounted on gaily caparisoned horses, and their bodies were painted as if ready for battle. They really presented a grand sight. I could hardly realize that so many Indians were upon us. I knew that if they were on the warpath that they would sweep the settlements and murder half the people before we could get sufficient help to repel them. I told my wife to take her baby and go and get in the canoe and cross the river and go to her father's as quick as she could. I took my rifle and boldly sallied out to meet the Indians. I was awful glad when they made signals of peace. They all rode around me, and I had to shake hands with them all. They said that they had come in to "make friends and be at peace and brothers forever with the brave Texans." They went on to Gonzales and made a treaty, which they regarded as sacred for many years. They camped one night around my house, and I went part of the way with them next day and sent a runner ahead to keep the people from being alarmed. They were great friends to the Texans, and were a great help to us. They were always after the wild Indians, and whenever they caught them they killed them. They were brave warriors in battle. On one occasion they wanted to make a raid into Mexico, and the war chief who was to lead the party

came to see me and Ben McCulloch and tried to persuade us
to go with them.

About ten days after the treaty I happened to go to
Gonzales, and I met a band of Lipan warriors coming into town
with the dead body of a Comanche. They were boiling over
with enthusiasm and singing their war songs. They were evidently anxious to show that they were executing the treaty with
a vengeance. They had quite a town just outside of Gonzales,
and their houses were constructed with no little skill.

As soon as the war party appeared the whole tribe rushed
out to meet them. Such rejoicing and such manifestations of
delight, courage, and welcome I never witnessed before. They
had fought the Comanches out on Brushy. It must have been
a drawn battle, but the Lipans declared they had won a great
victory, notwithstanding the fact that they had but one of the
dead bodies of their enemy. They had a great pow-wow, and
took every opportunity to show the dead warrior to the white
people and assure us that the Comanches would never dare to
trouble us again since we now had the brave Lipans for our
allies. They cut the warrior up into small pieces and put them
in pots and boiled them. They gave a particular portion of it to
the squaws, and they danced and sang around it for hours. They
had a great buffalo hide spread out in front of an old warrior's
tent, upon which some young men "beat a very nice tune,"
keeping time with the vocal music of the squaws. The old
warrior was very old and covered with scars. He would run out
of his tent and eat a mouthful of the Comanche, then a young
chief would hand him a long pipe and he would take just one
whiff and again retire to his tent. Then there would be more
music, and every soul of the five hundred joined in the terrible
singing. After that others tasted of the Comanche warrior, and
then the old chief appeared again. They offered me a choice
slice of the Comanche, but I politely informed them that I had
just eaten a rattlesnake and was too full to eat any more. This

made the chiefs laugh a great deal, and they patted me on the back and said something complimentary, I guess. They kept up their jubilee all night. In about ten days they broke camp and came along by Col. King's ranch.

From some cause there was a great deal of sickness among them. They camped near our place again, and the old war chief's wife died. His name was Francisco. He was a very large man, and the finest looking head I ever saw. There was no doubt but that he was a man of remarkable mental ability. He was well acquainted with Col. King, and they both spoke Spanish. He went to Col. King and told him that if he would bury his wife "American style" he would give him a fine horse. The old gentlemen took two or three negroes and went to the camp and dug a grave. Old Francisco sat in deep silence under the shade of a tree, with his arms folded, during the solemn ceremony of the interment. The tribe began to move while the body was being lowered in the grave. About twenty young warriors and subordinate chiefs remained and sat on the ground around the grand looking old man.

It was a remarkable sight. There were the black Africans lowering the dead queen in the earth; a tall white Anglo-Saxon directing the solemn rites, and the naked red warriors seated in silence not far away. What a lofty subject for the brush of one of the old masters.

As soon as the grave had been closed, the chief and his warriors arose and mounted their horses. Old Francisco bowed to Col. King like a royal king—and he looked every inch a king. Then they instantly shot away at full speed. They were all riding fine horses, and it seemed to me as though they rode like the wind.

Just as they rounded a point of the bluff I heard several shots, followed by a series of war-whoops. I rode up there to see what had happened, and, to my surprise, I found a dog, a mule, and a horse all lying on the ground, shot in the head. When I met them again I asked them why they killed the animals. They said: "For Francisco's wife to have something to ride in the next world and a dog to hunt for her."

I had much to do with these Indians for many years. There was something strange about them. They were different in many ways from any other Indians I ever saw. Their word was sacred to them, and it seemed to do them much good to do something for a friend. They would ride hundreds of miles to do a favor for a man they liked. They were the most faithful of allies and the most terrible of foes.

Chapter XIV.

CAPTURE OF CAPT. BIRD AND RUFE PERRY—HOMELINESS SAVES MR. CHISHOLM'S LIFE.

It was very seldom that the Comanches ever spared a life, but there is one instance to be recorded in their favor. Capt. Jim Bird, an old Texan, and Rufe Perry were camped on the Clato, about twenty-five miles from Gonzales. They were locating land. They had not seen any signs of Indians, and at that time there was not much fear of a raid from the red devils.

Just about sundown the two old veterans were in the act of lying down by their camp fire when about a hundred well mounted warriors dashed up to the fire. The white men thought they were Tonkaways, and they were so sure of it that they hardly felt inclined to rise up. Capt. Bird understood Spanish and Comanche, and he no sooner heard the first words uttered than he whispered: "My God, Rufe, they are Comanches."

The chief told them to get up, and he then stepped in front of Capt. Bird, whom he well knew, and said: "I will spare your lives on one condition. The Tonkaways are camped not far from here, and if you will show us their trail I will let you go. If you do not, I will skin you alive."

Capt. Bird was a brave and an honorable man. He did not like to betray his friends, the Tonkaways, but he thought that while they were hunting the trail he and his friend might get a chance to escape. He accordingly told the chief he would go with him. They made a circle of many miles without striking a trail. The old chief rode up to Bird and caught him by his collar and shook him. He placed his lance against his breast and savagely said: "I will give you one more chance, and if you don't find that trail I will run this lance through your heart."

They made another long ride, and, fortunately for the prisoners, they heard the low moaning voice of a Tonkaway squaw. She was doubtless cooing over her little baby.

The chief ordered them all to dismount at once. A reconnoitering party was sent forward, and they returned in a few minutes, reporting that they were within a few hundred yards of the enemy's camp.

Capt. Bird said he felt like a traitor, for he had no idea that the Comanche chief would keep his word and spare his life.

The chief mounted about twenty-five of his men on the best horses and rode away. In a short time he returned with four hundred Tonkaway horses—every one that the tribe had. It was a master stroke in Indian warfare. Not a dog barked, not a shot was fired.

The Comanches hurried forward towards the mountains, and when a few miles away the chief rode up to Capt. Bird and said, "Buena Hombre," and told him to go. Perry was in an ecstasy of delight, but Capt. Bird was silent and mortified with shame. The Tonkaways never recovered their horses.

About the time that the Comanches were trying to make a treaty with the Texans they spared another man's life. Old man Chisholm was a blacksmith at Old Washington. He was a funny little old man, and regarded by every one as the ugliest and most harmless man in the world. He was at Old Washington first, and was a great favorite with Gen. Houston and all other prominent men. He was a little dried-up old man, and would not have weighed much over a hundred pounds; but his muscles were of iron and his sinews of steel, while he had the heart of a lion.

After the capital had been moved from Old Washington, old man Chisholm, concluded he would go out West, where there was some chance of having a little fun occasionally. He had some fun. He was riding his old pony along the trail, headed for Col. King's ranch, when, suddenly looking around, he saw an army of warriors almost at his heels. He knew his old pony could not run, but he spurred him into a gallop and managed to keep ahead of his pursuers for two or three hundred yards. The warriors rode up on him and dragged him off of his horse and then cut his saddle off and threw it on the ground.

They began to jabber among themselves, little dreaming that he understood their language. All at once they began to clap their hands and laugh. One had said, "D—n him, he is too ugly to kill." Another said, "He is too ugly to eat; he would give an Indian the belly-ache." They danced around him and laughed a great deal. Finally they put him on his pony, bareback, with his face towards the animal's tail, and then two led the pony and the balance set up a shout and whipped him with quirts all the way to camp.

When they got into camp they all surrounded him and laughed as if they would kill themselves. They got an old silk plug hat and put it on him, and then they would pry open his eyes and blow in them and ask him how he came to be so awful ugly. Some said, "Maybe he is the devil." The squaws and the little Indians stuck arrows in him and said to him, "They won't hurt you; you are too ugly."

After they had exhausted themselves with laughter, the chief told the warriors that they might decide what should be done with the old man. There were twenty-five Comanches and fifteen Wacos in camp. The Wacos wanted to burn him, but the Comanches voted to spare his life. They still jokingly said that he was too ugly to kill, but the real fact was that the Comanches were becoming alarmed at the growing power of Texas, and they were afraid of being driven entirely out of the country, and they wanted to make a treaty of peace.

They had another frolic around old man Chisholm; the

Chapter XV.

PLUM CREEK.

The greatest battle that we ever had with the Comanches was the battle of Plum Creek. The generals of the little Texas army in this short campaign exhibited military ability of the very highest order, while the soldiers exposed themselves with reckless daring, and charged at the word of command like Grecian heroes. Every man did his duty.

The Comanches were greatly superior to us in number, but the battle was a crushing defeat, and was the end of the long reign of terror of these terrible red devils in Texas.

About five hundred Comanches, well armed and mounted on their best horses, slipped over the border and suddenly appeared in the vicinity of Victoria. They plundered and sacked the little town of Linnville and robbed every store and every house of everything valuable. Their dash into this part of the country was a complete surprise.

As the long column marched across the prairies it presented a ludicrous sight. The naked warriors had tried to dress themselves in the clothing they had stolen. Many of them put on cloth coats and buttoned them behind. Most of them had on stolen shoes and hats. They spread the calico over their horses, and tied hundreds of yards of ribbon in their horses' manes and to their tails. These Indians had been preparing for this raid for a long time. They all had new white shields, and many of the warriors had long tails to their headgear.

We got the news at Gonzales that a strong column of Comanches had passed into the lower country, and we at once got into the saddle and marched to the rescue of our friends. We camped at Isham Good's first, and, not hearing any news, we were about to return home, when Ben McCulloch rode into camp. Goat Jones was with him. They reported that the Indians had plundered the lower country, and were returning on the same trail. Capt. Caldwell asked me to take a good man and scout to the front and see if I could see anything of the Indians. I took John Baker, and we rode all night. About daylight we came in sight of the Indians, about seven miles from our camp. We rode back and reported.

During my absence Gen. Felix Huston had been elected to the command of the army, and Ed Burleson had joined us with about one hundred men, including some fifteen Tonkaways.

Gen. Huston asked me to take five picked men and ride to the front and select a good position to make the attack. I came in sight of them. They were on the prairie, and the column looked to be seven miles long. Here I witnessed a horrible sight. A captain and one man rode in among the Indians. The captain escaped, but I saw the Indians kill the private. I ordered my men to keep at a safe distance and pick off an Indian as the opportunity presented.

We skirmished with them for about two miles, when our army came up in line and opened fire. It looked as if we were taking desperate chances, for I am sure that we only had 202 men, but every man was a veteran. Gen. Huston deserves great credit for the courage he displayed in this battle. He rode right with the line, and never flinched under the most galling fire.

At the first volley the Indians became demoralized, and it was easy to see that we had them beat. Just as we rode against them I received a bullet in the thigh. It made a terrible wound, and the blood ran until it sloshed out of my boots. I was compelled to dismount, or rather I fell off of my horse. After a moment I felt better and made an effort to rejoin the line of battle. I met an Indian, and was just in the act of shooting him when he threw up his hands and shouted "Tonkaway!"

While on the skirmish line, an Indian dashed at Mr. Smitzer with a lance. I fired right in the Indian's face and knocked him off his horse, but I did not kill him. However, I got the fine hat he had stolen.

While I was scrambling about, trying to staunch the blood that was flowing from my leg, I came across a great big fat negro woman, who was hiding in the grass. She no sooner saw me than she exclaimed: "Bless God, here is a white man once more." Her little child was hiding in the grass just like a frightened animal. If it had been big enough it would have run from me like a deer.

Not far from the old negro I found the body of Mrs. Crosby. There were two arrows in her body. They had passed clear through her. She was just gasping in death. She had been a prisoner, and the red devils had killed her when they saw they were defeated.

A little further on I found Mrs. Watts. They had shot an arrow at her breast, but her steel corset saved her life. It had entered her body, but Isham Good and I fastened a big pocket knife on the arrow and pulled it out. She possessed great fortitude, for she never flinched, though we could hear the breastbone crack when the arrow came out. She turned over on her side and bled a great deal, but she soon recovered. She was the wife of a custom house officer, and I think her maiden name was Ewing.

She asked for poor Mrs. Crosby and told us that the Indians whipped the poor woman frequently and called her a "peon," because she could not read. They had stolen several books, and when in camp at night they would gather around Mrs. Watts and ask her to explain the pictures and read to them. Mrs. Watts' husband had been killed when the Indians sacked Linnville. She afterwards married Dr. Fretwell, and resided in

Port Lavaca.

It has always been a mystery to me why the Indians became so terribly demoralized in this battle. It was fought on the open prairie, and they could easily see that they greatly outnumbered us. It is rather strange that they did not make a stand. It was one of the prettiest sights I ever saw in my life. The warriors flourished their white shields, and the young chiefs galloped about the field with the long tails streaming from their hats and hundreds of vari-colored ribbons floating in the air, exhibiting great bravado. Some of them dashed courageously very close to us, and two or three of them lost their lives in this foolhardy display of valor.

Our boys charged with a yell and did not fire until they got close to the enemy. The Indians were panic stricken, and fled at once. The Texans followed them over the prairies for fifteen or twenty miles.

That night, around the camp-fire, many strange stories were told. One of the strangest was of an old black chief, whose head looked as if it had been nearly blown off. He gripped the horn of his saddle with his hands, and dozens of the boys declared that they struck him on the head with the butt of their muskets as they passed him. No blow could make him release his hold. Though dead and stiff, he remained on his war-horse. There was a good deal of talk of it at the time. I had almost forgotten the incident when I read the story of the headless rider of Woerth. This occurred during the Franco-German war. Newspaper readers will remember that a French colonel had his head shot off with a cannon ball, but he did not fall from his horse. The furious animal galloped about over the field during the whole battle, carrying on his back the headless colonel. Scientists talked and wrote about the affair and offered some sort of an explanation. I think they said that the muscles in death became so rigid that no earthly power could cause them to relax. This must have been the case with the old Indian, for dozens of truthful men declared that he was as dead as a door nail, but that he still clung to his horse. The horse ran off in the woods with him, and his body was never found.

From the best information I could gather I think the boys killed about forty of the Comanches. We lost not a man, but seven were wounded: Robert Hall, Henry McCulloch, Arch Gibson, Columbus DeWitt, Dr. Smitzer, and two others, whose names I don't remember.

The Tonkaways brought in the dead body of a Comanche warrior, and they built a big fire not far from where I was lying. My wound had begun to pain me considerably, and I did not pay much attention to them for some time. After awhile they began to sing and dance, and I thought that I detected the odor of burning flesh. I raised up and looked around, and, sure enough, our allies were cooking the Comanche warrior. They cut him into slices and broiled him on sticks. Curiously enough the eating of the flesh acted upon them as liquor does upon other men. After a few mouthfuls they began to act as if they were very drunk, and I don't think there was much pretense or sham about it. They danced, raved, howled and sang, and invited me to get up and eat a slice of Comanche. They said it would make me brave. I was very hungry, but not sufficiently so to become a cannibal. The Tonkaways were wild over the victory, and they did not cease their celebration until sunrise.

The boys captured the war chief's cap. It was a peculiar affair, made of the finest of furs, and it had a tail attached to it at least thirty feet long. Several other fine caps were picked up on the field.

About fifteen miles from Plum Creek the soldiers heard a child crying in a thicket. All were afraid that the noise was some ruse of the Indians to induce the Texans into an ambush, but finally one fool fellow declared that he would go in and see what it was. He found a little child, a boy, lying on the leaves by itself. The soldier brought it out, and it proved to be a child of the head chief of the Comanches. They brought it to camp, and old Judge Bellinger adopted it. The little Indian did not live but three or four months.

We captured the Indian pack train. The mules were loaded with household furniture, wearing apparel, and general merchandise. There were five hundred of these pack mules. The government had just received a supply of stores at Linnville, and the Indians had captured these. We hardly knew what to do with all this stuff, and we finally concluded to divide it among ourselves. Some days after I reached home the boys sent me a pack mule and a pack. In the pack there was a pillow and a bolster of home-made cloth and considerable dry goods. There were also coverlets, sheets, quilts, and clothing. If I had known who the stuff belonged to I would have, of course, returned it.

After some days my friends got an old buggy and hitched an old horse to it and made an effort to get me home. At the crossing of the San Marcos the old horse balked and refused to pull the vehicle up the hill. That made me mad, and I got out of the buggy and walked on home. I was tired and hungry, and I wanted to see Polly and get something to eat and have her dress my wound. Polly was glad to see me, for she thought I was dead. Old man King had gone home, and, from some cause, he had carried my shoes. He told Polly I would be home in a few days, but during the evening she found my shoes, full of blood, and she began to scream and upbraid her father. He then had to tell her the truth, but he insisted that I was only slightly wounded. Polly did not believe him, but when she saw me walking home she ran to meet me and declared that she never intended to let me go to fight Indians any more.

This battle was fought on the 12th of August, 1840.

Chapter XVI.

A HARMLESS MEXICAN ARMY IN TEXAS.

In the spring of 1840* we had a scare that I have never seen mentioned in history. All at once the story reached us at Gonzales that a Mexican army had captured San Antonio. Two or three citizens were at once sent to San Antonio to see what had happened. These men returned in a few days and reported that the republic had certainly been invaded. They said that they could see hundreds of Mexican troops, in their bright uniforms, right in the streets of San Antonio. This was true. A daring Mexican general by the name of Vasquez, at the head of about 800 soldiers, had made a dash across the Rio Grande and captured the city of San Antonio without firing a shot. This man acted very strangely for a Mexican officer. He never harmed any one or made any prisoners. After remaining in San Antonio a few days he wheeled about and resumed his march to Mexico.

When the people learned that an army of 800 Mexican regulars were in San Antonio there was no limit to the alarm that spread over the frontier. Were we to have another San Jacinto campaign? Our regular army had been disorganized, and our only hope for protection lay in the militia and minute men. Such men as myself, Col. King, McCulloch and Caldwell concluded that this was merely the vanguard of a large Mexican

---

*   The year was actually 1842 [Editor].

army, and we realized that it would take some time to organize a force capable of fighting even 800 Mexican regulars. We concluded that it would be best to move our families out on the Colorado and then come back and organize a force to meet the enemy. I hurried back from the Colorado at once and joined the troops at Gonzales. We marched in the direction of San Antonio, and, to our utmost surprise, we learned that the Mexican general had evacuated the city.

This military operation on the part of the enemy was a puzzle to us all. Some thought that the Mexican general had fallen back and formed a junction with a larger army, and that we would next hear their cannon thundering on the Brazos. A considerable army gathered in the vicinity of San Antonio, and we remained in camp about three months, but never heard from the enemy. The Mexican general must have simply been exercising his troops. He was certainly not hunting a battle.

When I look back and think of the constant alarms and the wars we had, the wonder is that we did not abandon the country. It is a greater wonder that the women were willing to stay in a wilderness where they were at any time liable to be murdered by Mexicans or tortured at the stake by merciless Indians. No pen will ever be able to do justice to the courage, patriotism, and devotion of the women who stood by their brothers, fathers, husbands, and sweethearts, while they were repelling the Mexicans, destroying the Indians, killing the snakes, and building the roads in the wilderness of Texas.

Chapter XVII.

BEAR HUNTING—BEAR KINGS.

In the spring of 1839 I rode up the Capotes, hunting bear. I had five splendid dogs, and I thought a great deal of them. We were out of meat, and I was anxious to kill a deer or a bear. Suddenly I heard the dogs barking and I rode up to them. To my utter astonishment they had a monster panther treed. I raised my old flint-lock and it made a long fire—"blowed," as we said in those days. The panther fell out of the tree and began to fight my dogs. I saw that he would soon kill all my fine dogs, so I drew a long Wilson Bowie knife from my belt and entered the fight myself. He had already ripped open one of my best hounds. I was very mad, and I rushed in and drove the knife clear through his heart. I shall never forget the vicious look in his magnificent yellow eyes. His great limbs fell powerless by his side, and I could not help admiring his wonderful beauty. He was nine feet from tip to tip, and was the largest panther ever killed in Texas.

It has been said that there are no leopards in America, but all old Texans know very well that if what was called a jaguar were put in a cage by the side of an Asiatic leopard, no man could tell one from the other. Our jaguar, or cougar, or Texas leopard attacked and killed buffalo and Texas bulls. There are but few now in Texas, but I presume they are still to be found in the mountains of Mexico.

I went on and struck a Waco trail. I put my feet by the side of the Indian tracks and I could not tell which was the freshest. I easily saw that there were ten or twelve warriors in the party.

I instantly returned home, and my wife asked me where the bear was. I did not want her to know there were Indians in the country, and I told her a little white lie—not often I told Polly a lie. In fact, she was the other part of myself, and she nearly always knew when I left the line of truth in the least little bit.

Again I went on the waters of the Sandies. I saw plenty of deer, but I wanted a fat one. I was riding a race horse called Wild Bill. I was not afraid of the Indians catching me on this horse. I killed a fat buck and dressed him and tied him to my saddle. The country out there was alive with wild mustangs. I started home with my buck and I came upon a dead horse. I rode up to the carcass and saw at a glance that the Indians had killed it only a few hours before for food. I knew the warriors were not far away, and I kept a sharp lookout. Pretty soon I saw a little smoke curling toward the skies. Almost before I knew it I rode in sight of the Indian camp. There sat about twenty-five warriors around the fire, broiling the mustang. Their horses were saddled and near the camp-fire. They saw me and sprang into their saddles and raised a war-whoop. I was not at all alarmed, for I knew my horse could outrun anything they had. I easily rode away from them, and never cut the buck loose from my saddle.

After resting a few days I took my little brother-in-law, who was about 12 years old, and went up on the San Marcos to kill bear. We were hunting around in the bends near where Luling now stands, and I thought I saw a flock of turkeys in a berry patch. We were slipping cautiously up to the little cluster of bushes when, to my utter astonishment, I saw seven Indian warriors, armed with short guns and bows and arrows. I whispered to the boy to stand still, but when I looked around he was flying. Just then the dogs jumped a deer, and I never heard hounds yelp so loud in my life. I ran on and caught up with the boy. I expected the Indians to pursue us, and I intended to give them a fight and die with the boy if necessary. Say, don't you think Napoleon would have made me a general if I had been in his army? I am sure that under fire I was just as cool and undisturbed as Junot or Lannes. I intended to go into a thicket and fight the enemy from ambush, but they never followed us. We went to Jim Foster's that night and reported about the Indians. Nothing more, however, was heard of these Indians.

I lived on the west side of the Guadalupe, twelve miles above Gonzales, and my nearest neighbor was the De Witt family, twelve miles away. These were the noted De Witts who obtained a grant from the Mexican government in 1825 to settle 400 families in Texas. The founder of the family and the originator of the scheme was named Green De Witt. He was a brave man and possessed executive ability of a high order. His surveyor was a man by the name of James Kerr. He was a member of the Missouri Senate and resigned his seat to help colonize Texas.

A few days after I reached home some one called our attention from the other side of the river. My little girl Elizabeth, then about four years old, went down to the canoe landing, and she returned and told me that the Indians had taken all of Uncle Jim Foster's horses, and they wanted me to come at once. I was in the saddle in a few minutes and I got Alse Miller and English Baker to go with me. We struck the trail and pursued the thieves to the mountains. I concluded that we were not strong enough to attack the Indian camp. There were only four of us, and there might have been a thousand of the Comanches. We reluctantly returned home.

There were a great many bear on the Oliver league, and in the fall hundreds of them were busy lapping the pecan trees. When I got up there it looked as if a cyclone had passed over the country. The bear would tear off the limbs and drag them to the ground, where they could devour the nuts at leisure. The whole face of the earth was covered with brush, and the trees looked as if they had just been swept by a storm. I had only one dog. He struck a big bunch of bear and bayed one. I shot the bear on the bank of the river. I thought I had given him a dead shot, but I jumped on him and we both rolled into the river. He was the largest long legged bear I ever saw. The water struck me to the armpits. While in the water the bear breathed his last, and I swam across the river and tied my bear with a grapevine to the shore. I went home and got a wagon and yoke of oxen. I had no help and had great trouble in getting the bear loaded. It was all the oxen could do to pull him ashore. Then I cut skids and made the oxen pull the bear on the wagon. He was one of the fattest and finest bear that I ever killed. I actually believe that there were between fifty and one hundred bear in that pecan forest. I wonder how many people know that bears have a leader, a king, if you please? This old fellow is an absolute autocrat, and he moves the flock or tribe from place to place. The Indians are familiar with this fact, though it escaped Mr. Darwin. Again, I went coon hunting in the Tonkaway bend. The dog treed something under the roots of a big walnut tree right on the bluff on the river bank. I patted the dog and he ran into the hole. When he got into the hole I heard him give an awful yell. He turned to get out, but a big bear had caught him behind. I caught the dog's head and pulled him out of the hole. He was the worst scared dog I ever saw. He ran off up the bottom and howled as if the devil were after him. I fired both barrels of my gun into the hole, but I don't think I hit him. By this time Col. King's dogs came to me. The bear ran on the bank of the bluff and I shot again, but I did not hurt him much. He fell over on his back and I was sure he was dead, and fearing that he would roll into the river, I jumped on him. The bear was very much alive and awfully in evidence. He hugged me at once as I had never been hugged before, and would have crushed the life out of me if the dogs had not come to my rescue. I loaded one barrel of my gun with a big rifle ball and placed the muzzle

Photo courtesy of The Center for American History, The University of Texas at Austin

Robert Hall exhibit at the 1936 Texas Centennial Exposition in Dallas.

right behind his fore shoulder and killed him dead. My brothers-in-law, John and Tom King, heard the noise of the battle and they galloped up on the other side of the river. There was about an 8-foot rise in the river at the time. The bear rolled right off in the river. I stripped myself. It was at night and I could see the black spot in the river. I plunged into the water and seized the bear by the foot and swam ashore with him. It was a monster and awful fat. The boys went after a wagon and hauled the animal to Col. King's. There was great rejoicing over the slaughter of this animal for we needed his flesh.

Chapter XVIII.

PAINT CALDWELL A PRISONER.

President Lamar concluded that he wanted to open up some sort of communication and trade with Santa Fe, and he sent Capt. Paint Caldwell with about one hundred men to that far away city. This was very a very strange piece of diplomacy. Caldwell was one of the most remarkable men that ever lived. He had a heart of gold, and the word fear conveyed no meaning to his soul. In open violation of every principle of international comity and courtesy, the whole force was made to surrender as prisoners of war in the city of Santa Fe. They were never treated as prisoners of war. Most of the men were loaded with chains and thrown into dungeons. After some time they were started on the long march to the City of Mexico on foot. In a few days the burning sun and the scorching sand began to crush the poor worn out prisoners. One who understood the Spanish language heard an officer say to the guards, "If the Americano diablos drop in the road, cut their throats as you would a dog, and bring me their ears that I may account for my prisoners." This act of butchery and inhumanity was performed several times. One day Capt. Caldwell himself fell in the road on the hot sand. A Mexican officer more humane than the others had become attached to the brave old veteran, and he bent over the prostrate and as he thought dying soldier and whispered: "If you desire I will cut your ears off and report you dead. Possibly you may hobble to some ranch and survive." The old captain could not bear the idea of losing his ears, and he struggled to his feet and rejoined his miserable comrades. I think he was gone about eighteen months. The Mexican government released these prisoners, but made them swear that they would never again bear arms against Mexico. Capt. Caldwell got home just in time to participate in the battle of the Salado. He regarded the oath that he had taken under duress as nothing, but always said that he never intended to surrender again to any Mexican soldiers.

Chapter XIX.

THE TERRIBLE BATTLE OF THE MEDINA, AND THE BATTLE OF SALADO.

General Toledo, when he was an ambassador to the court of Naples, often insisted that he had participated in one of the greatest battles that the world ever saw. When his cheeks were reddened with a little wine, he would declare that with ten thousand such Texans as he led against the Mexican lines at the Medina, he could ride all over Europe. The Medina was indeed a terrible affair. The Mexicans were commanded by the only general of any ability who had ever led an army into Texas. This man's name was Aredondo. He commanded about 4000 regular troops. Halting about six miles south of the Medina, he threw up breastworks in the form of an angle, with the opening towards San Antonio. The Texans had whipped the Mexicans so often that they had come to the conclusion that a handful of Texans could march all over Mexico. Eight hundred and fifty Americans stood in line of battle and eagerly demanded to be lead against the enemy. Their commander, Don Jose Alvarez Toledo, a Cuban by birth, but the descendant of a noble Spanish family, suspected a stratagem of some kind, and he was in favor of maneuvering for another position before making the attack; but the Americans declared that nothing would satisfy them but an order to charge. And charge they did. The Mexicans fled at first as if panic stricken, but when the whole American army was inside of the angle, suddenly up rose two walls of steel and blazing fire. There was a roar of cannon, a rattle of musketry, a hurrah, and then the smoke cleared away, and there stood only 93 Texans. Toledo ordered a retreat. Even this little handful, in the jaws of death, shouted, "We never retreat." Toledo, Perry, Taylor and Bullard escaped.

The chronicler of Texas events has many strange events to record, but none as astounding as the conflict at the Medina. Some years afterwards a patriot buried the bones of the Americans, and nailed to a large oak a tablet which bore the inscription, "Here lie the braves, who, imitating the immortal example of Leonidas, sacrificed their fortunes and lives contending against tyrants."

I have talked with men who were in this battle, and we have often around our camp fires compared this terrible affair with the battle of Salado which occurred twenty-nine years afterwards. In the Salado the Mexicans were commanded by the veteran French general, Woll, who boasted that he had learned the science of war under Marshal Soult. He commanded 1200 regular troops. Nearly all historians claim that we had 300 Texans on the field, but I am positive that our force has been over estimated. Our commander, old Paint Caldwell, was equal to a thousand men. No man who ever stood on Texas soil was his equal in battle. As soon as the bullets began to whistle he seemed to grow taller and look grander. I don't think it ever occurred to him that he might be hit. He rode over a battlefield as unconcerned as if he had been out cornshucking. His nerves must have been made of iron; nothing disturbed him. This battle occurred on the 18th of September, 1842.

They got news in San Antonio of the advance of Gen. Woll, and Jack Hays was sent out on the Laredo road to watch the enemy. Hays missed Gen. Woll's column entirely. The strategetic old rascal had made a new road from the Rio Grande to San Antonio, and fell upon the city like a flash of lightning. District Court was in session, and he captured the court and all the lawyers and sent them off as prisoners to the dungeons of Mexico. The news reached us at Gonzales, and we at once fell into line. Capt. Caldwell himself came to my house after me. I joined him next day. He was camped on a creek about eighteen miles northeast of San Antonio. Hays joined us that night. The next day we organized and old Paint Caldwell was elected commander of the army. He at once sent Jack Hays forward to select a battlefield. Hays selected a crossing on the Salado, about two miles above where the "Sunset" road crosses. About midnight we took up the line of march, keeping away from the road. We came in sight of the enemy about daylight. We were awful hungry, and French Smith ran a fat cow into camp and shot her down. While we were skinning and broiling beef we heard the rattle of Jack Hays' musketry. He had already engaged the enemy. Old Sol Simmons was a large man and a powerful eater. He was terrible hungry, and he had a dozen big pieces of the fat cow on the fire. When the firing commenced he swallowed the big pieces of meat without chewing it. Capt. Caldwell ordered the horses tied in the bottom, and the men formed in line of battle. Jack Hays had joined us by this time. The Mexicans appeared in front. There was a skirmish at a distance of about 600 yards. Old Sol Simmons, who was still swallowing beef, was the first man hit. He roared that he was a dead man, and began to throw up that beef. It looked as if he had enough cow inside of him to have killed him. He was hit in the stomach and the bullet was never found, yet the man got well. The Mexican infantry and artillery advanced and took up a position on a slight elevation. We heard the rattle of musketry and cannon east of us. We could not imagine what was going on. We afterwards learned that Capt. Dawson, with forty-five men, was trying to cut his way through the Mexican lines. The world knows the story: They were all massacred. I think Alse Miller and a man named Moods* escaped. Caldwell put me over in the

---

*   Gonzalvo Woods [Editor].

and fire while the other loaded. Old Parson Carroll, a Methodist preacher, would step up on the bank and fire, and shout "God take your souls." Caldwell sent me up the creek to see if there was an attempt to surround us. I climbed up a tree and saw a Mexican slipping on another scout named Hill. I got my gun and shot at him. He dropped over on the horn of his saddle. We found him next day seated against a tree with the gun across his lap. It was one of the finest rifles I ever saw.

I heard a general advance and I went under the bank and leaned against a little pecan tree. The tree I first picked out to protect me was shot entirely off by a cannon shot. The Mexicans came up within forty yards of our lines, cavalry, infantry and artillery. Our boys stood firm. One column under Old Cordova advanced upon us along a ravine that intersected the creek. Willis Randall shot and killed Old Cordova. He was a Nacogdoches Spaniard and we all knew him. We killed and wounded a great many of the enemy when they made the general advance. The Mexicans fell back.

That night the moon was shining very brightly. A soldier named Conn and I went out in front on the battlefield and we found that the enemy had fallen back on San Antonio. We found a great many dead and wounded. We camped on the field and the next day we received news that Gen. Woll had evacuated San Antonio and was making a forced march toward the Rio Grande. We went around the head of the San Antonio river and struck Gen. Woll's trail. Reinforcements were joining us every hour, until we were about six hundred strong. Gen. Woll crossed the Medina and halted on a splendid natural position. The two armies were in sight of each other for two days, and strangely enough the Texans did not attack the enemy. I think there were about a half a dozen men who wanted to have command of the army, and they were constantly caucusing and trying in some way to remove old Paint Caldwell. Woll began to retreat again. We skirmished with his rear guard. Jack Hays command of the army, and they were constantly caucusing and trying in some way to remove old Paint Caldwell. Woll began to retreat again. We skirmished with his rear guard. Jack Hays charged a column of Mexicans, but suffered a repulse from lack of proper support. Our officers constantly differed with each other, and many wanted to play the general; consequently Gen. Woll marched away from us. Big Foot Wallace was in this battle, and Creed Taylor was badly wounded in the hand. I saw a man named Lucky shot through the body. I was sure he was killed, but he recovered. This ended the affair of the Salado, but it was not the end of Woll's invasion. A large force gathered on the Rio Grande and attacked the town of Mier. Everybody knows the story of the Mier prisoners. Col. Seguin, a Mexican gentleman who had been prominent in Texas, went away with Gen. Woll. I don't think the Texans treated Seguin right. Henry McCulloch was in the battle of the Salado.

This was the last time that Mexican troops were ever seen in San Antonio.

Photo courtesy of Lynn Glenewinkle

Front view of Robert Hall in his "frontiersman's suit."

Chapter XX.

MASSACRE OF FANNIN'S MEN.

After the massacre of Fannin's men Santa Anna's good fortune deserted him, and from that hour his career, steeped in crime and blood, began to tend toward the destruction of his ambitious schemes. No doubt Gen. Urrea intended to treat Fannin and his men as prisoners of war, but Santa Anna's bloodthirsty soul revolted at the idea of sparing the life of any American. He no sooner learned that Urrea had captured a considerable force of Texans then he ordered them all to be shot. He afterwards declared that he did not understand at the time that they had surrendered as prisoners of war, and to Gen. Houston he tried to excuse himself for the wholesale murder on the grounds that the Mexican Supreme Court had passed a law ordering that all Americans found in arms in Texas should be treated as pirates. "I declare you, General, upon the honor of a soldier," said Santa Anna, "that I did not know that Fannin had surrendered, and I promise that if I ever live to get Urrea in my hands I will have him shot for his treachery."

"You are the dictator, and without any superior; you, Gen. Santa Anna, are the government of Mexico," replied Gen. Houston.

Gen. Houston had ordered both Fannin and Travis to blow up the forts they occupied and retreat into the interior, where he was forming a line of defense. Poor Fannin was a brave man, but, either influenced by his contempt for the Mexican or lack of generalship, he displayed little or no military ability. He camped at a point where the Mexicans easily secured that advantage of the ground. He was no sooner attacked than all saw that they had made a great mistake. There was no water in the camp, and the cannon soon became useless. They fought like heroes, and when Fannin saw that all was lost he displayed courage of the very highest order. He went himself to Urrea's tent and arranged the terms of surrender. They were simply to be treated as prisoners of war and allowed to return to their homes in Georgia as soon as possible. No one ever dreamed that these terms would be violated. A few men escaped the butchery. Judge Hunter was one of them. I have seen and talked with several others. It was the blood of the Alamo and the blood of Fannin's men that purchased the independence of Texas.

In my long career I have noticed that murderers, desperadoes and thieves never prosper. Their deviltry always overtakes them, though sometimes they do not suffer until their locks are white.

THE ANNEXATION

When the war was over, our people began to discuss annexation to the United States. I was opposed to annexation, and voted first, last, and all the time for the Lone Star. About the time Gen. Taylor entered Texas at the head of a United States army, orders came for us to form a company and locate at San Marcos. We soon raised about seventy-five men. Henry McCulloch and I ran for captain. He beat me five votes. I served as a private. We looked for a long time for an officer to come and muster us into service. Finally, we saw old Major Fontleroy coming with two or three soldiers. Jack Hodges, who is still living, concluded to play a joke on the old warrior, and he seized his gun and went out on the road and halted him. The major took it all in good part and complimented us for our vigilance. He mustered us into service. I stayed there about a month and never saw any signs of Indians or an enemy. An immense catfish used to swim up to where we threw crumbs into the river. I frequently jumped into the water and caught him by the tail, but could never hold him. He would often turn and charge me. I got a bayonet and dived down into the water and drove it into his back. The bayonet broke, and the boys said he went up the river like a race horse. We never saw him again.

About this time Ben McCulloch received orders from Gen. Taylor to raise a picked company of about thirty mounted men for service as spies and scouts in Mexico. I joined this company, but furnishing a substitute for my old company. We marched to San Antonio and stayed a short time. There I bought the finest bowie knife I ever saw. It cost me twenty-five dollars. I carried it in my bosom during the whole war. I knew the Mexican soldiery well, and was familiar with the peculiar tactics of their scouts in throwing a lasso over the heads of their enemies. Many of our men in Mexico were captured and dragged to death in this way.

We followed the old San Antonio road to Laredo. There was not a house on the road. Just at the crossing of the San Miguel we met old man Level. He is still living. He was carrying dispatches for Lamar to San Antonio. He told us that a comrade named Johnson had been traveling with him. They camped at South Lake. During the night they heard a great deal of noise that puzzled them. Early in the morning Johnson said he would go on and kill a deer. In a few moments Level heard firing, and he soon saw that the Indians had killed his comrade. Level escaped with his dispatches and he was awful glad to meet us. We marched on and when near the lake we saw a smoke. We left the road and McCulloch placed his men in a thicket and asked me to go with him and bring on the fight. We crept cautiously up near the fire, and to our surprise and joy we recognized Capt. Lamar's company of Texas troops. They had heard of the murder and were out looking for the Indians. We found part of Johnson's body. The wolves had torn it to fragments. We gathered up all we could of our poor comrade, and buried his bones on the lonely prairie. We then marched on to Laredo.

A large side-wheel steamboat was lying at Laredo. She stayed about a year before there was water enough for her to get away. We crossed the Rio Grande and camped in Old Mexico, about fifteen miles below Laredo. Here we saw the greatest turkey roosts that I ever saw in my life. Every little mesquite was black with the fine birds for miles. At Salado we crossed on a little ferry, and here I got very much vexed at the whole command. There was a dance in the little Mexican town, and all the boys, including Ben McCulloch, went to it, leaving me to guard the camp and horses. I was very mad. We were in the enemy's country, and I did not approve of any such foolishness. I stayed in the camp, but told the boys that if the Indians attacked me I did not intend to fire a gun.

From there we marched rapidly on until we reached Monterey. We stopped one day and joined the army at Saltillo the next day. About thirty miles from Saltillo we passed through some of the grandest, most beautiful, and lofty scenery I ever saw. In the valley, which was well watered and irrigated, there were beautiful groves of trees and fine orchards loaded with fruit. There were some fine houses here and the people were very hospitable and clever. We had to cross a magnificent range of mountains. The ascent was very steep, and a misstep would have sent our horses rolling thousands of feet below into the valley. Upon one occasion the sun was shining bright on our column, but we looked down into the valley below us and saw a thunder cloud. We were above it. The rain was pouring out of it, and the deep thunder was rolling and echoing through the mountains, while the lightning almost blinded us. It was a magnificent sight. At Saltillo, Gen. Churchill mustered us into service, and we went into camp about twenty-five miles from Saltillo, in one of the prettiest valleys I ever saw. Gen. Taylor

Photo courtesy of Lynn Glenewinkle
Back view of Robert Hall in his "frontiersman's suit."

was glad to see us. His splendid little army was camped in the valley. There was meanness and treachery at work somewhere against Gen. Taylor. The authorities were constantly stripping him of his men. I think somebody was jealous of the military fame that Gen. Taylor was winning with his little army on the plains of Mexico. All knew that Santa Anna was coming against us with an immense army; and yet, instead of sending us reinforcements, they were constantly ordering us to send our best regiments to the support of points where there was no enemy. Possibly somebody was afraid that another victory would make Gen. Taylor president. No other man on earth but Gen. Taylor, after his regiments had been taken away from him, would have made a stand at Buena Vista. We fought two enemies at Buena Vista—the people who were trying to ruin Gen. Taylor, and Santa Anna—and we were victorious, in spite of the singular combination against us and the greatest army that Mexico ever put in the field.

Chapter XXI.

STORIES OF BUENA VISTA.

Some days before the battle of Buena Vista, Gen. Taylor selected a part of our company to advance into the enemy's country. Ben McCulloch led us. We went eighty miles to the front. In about four miles of Encarnacion we saw a fire. Ben McCulloch and Captain Howard captured an old Mexican cavalry soldier. We turned him over to Jim Groce, who had been a Mier prisoner. We went on a little piece and saw a fellow cut loose from a Spanish dagger. We asked our prisoner what that meant. He replied, "Quien sabe!" He had already sworn on his life that there were no Mexican troops in Encarnacion. We went along a mile further. I heard the words from a Mexican mouth, "Quien vive?" Then a whole platoon fired at us. Our horses plunged, but we conquered them and charged on into Santa Anna's lines. There was a terrible rattling of drums in his camp. We whirled, and Ben McCulloch put Lieutenant Kelly and myself in the rear, and we galloped on. We rode about fifteen miles, watching the enemy. Then we rode leisurely into Gen. Taylor's camp and reported that Santa Anna was in full force right in our front. The Mexican spy jerked away from Groce and escaped during the skirmish. The next day Gen. Taylor asked us to go to the front again. We rode in the mountains and watched Santa Anna's columns with spy glasses. They had at least a thousand women and a thousand dogs with them. We watched the moving column and reported to Gen. Taylor. Gen. Taylor fell back from his old camp to Buena Vista.

The San Juan creek was a dry creek, and only ran when it

rained. It was a difficult place for military operations. The Washington battery came into position. Santa Anna could not advance down that road without meeting the Washington battery. It was well fortified. Next morning about 8 o'clock Santa Anna's columns came in sight. There seemed to be no end to the long lines of glittering infantry and cavalry. Bragg's battery was put on one of the hills. The Mexicans sent 1000 cavalry to attack our rear. They were sure of victory. Ben McCulloch came to me and told me to go to the front and watch. I went between the two lines and directly Ben came to me and told me they needed me at the Washington battery. I went, and found young Crittenden, one of old Taylor's aides. They wanted me at once to go and carry Gen. Taylor's reply to Santa Anna. Santa Anna had demanded a surrender. I carried Taylor's dispatches to Santa Anna; then we came back. Taylor sent another dispatch. We handed these to Santa Anna, and as we rode back towards the Washington battery Santa Anna fired a signal gun. The battle had opened. The Mexican band began to play. It was the loveliest music I ever heard in my life. Then Gen. Ampudia with about 12,000 men passed in the mountains above us. Col. Bowles, with his Indiana troops, was in the valley below. Ampudia descended upon the Indiana troops in the morning and they ran like the devil. Some Mexican cavalry cut their way around the mountains to Ampudia. They aimed to get in our rear. We were ordered with the dragoons and with two pieces of artillery we flew to the field of Buena Vista. There was one company in a corral, and the Mexicans had charged them. We ran there with the artillery and we shelled the enemy as they retreated. I mean Ben McCulloch's company and the dragoons, 400 in number, and two pieces of artillery. We drove them over the mountains. While there I saw the enemy kill Col. Yell, of Arkansas, and his men scattered everywhere. I heard a young fellow hallooing for help. A Mexican was chasing him with a lance. He was in big luck: he jerked the lance out of the

Mexican's hands and killed him. It was the finest lance I ever saw. I offered him $25 for it, but he said he would not take a hundred. An officer ran right by us and we fired at him. He ran to us and offered his sword. He was a fine looking fellow. Then we wheeled right around and went against old Ampudia with infantry and artillery. The first thing we saw was a white flag. We hurrahed then. Taylor had sent Crittenden with a white flag and asked them to surrender. We did not know that, and could have easily captured the whole command. Gen. Taylor here made a mistake. They easily joined Santa Anna. That night they shelled us all night. Just a little before day we got a bite to eat. They did a good deal of shelling during the morning. They had a very large cannon up in the mountains, and with this gun they could reach any part of the field. Our artillery replied furiously. About noon Santa Anna advanced his whole line. They looked like a black cloud. Taylor took a part of the Washington battery and put it with the Bragg battery on the ridge. The dragoons were placed in the rear of Bragg's battery, out of the line of fire. Jeff Davis and Col. Hardin and young Clay were located on the road in the foothills. Our batteries opened with balls. Finally they got near enough for our boys to use grape shot. Gen. Taylor sat on his white horse right by the battery, and we could hear him say, "Give them a little more grape, boys." I knew what we were there for. I felt like a wild hog. My hair pushed my hat off more than once. The batteries swept lanes through the enemy's lines. They repulsed the whole Mexican army. Col. Jeff Davis, Hardin and young Clay charged the Mexican infantry. Hardin and young Clay both fell. The Mexicans gave way. Everybody on that field felt that to Jeff Davis belonged the palm of victory. We all heard that the next day Gen. Taylor sent for him and offered him his hand, saying, "My daughter was a better judge of men than I am." They were ever after warm friends.

All was quiet on the battle field at night save the wails of the wounded. About 4 o'clock next morning McCulloch's company was ordered to the front again. We saw that Santa Anna had retreated. It was an awful sight; the field was now covered with dead and wounded Mexicans. The wounded were moaning bitterly. We turned up into a ravine and struck a whole company of Mexicans. They sprang up to fight us, but we charged them and made them surrender. We took the flints out of their guns and marched them to Gen. Taylor's headquarters. They did not know that Santa Anna had retreated. We still advanced, and I threw my gun on a nice looking little Mexican, and he ran, fell on his knees and surrendered. I jumped down and kicked him and told him to vamoose to camp. I met an ambulance; one tire was off. I looked in it, and it was full of feet, legs, and hands. I returned and we reported to Gen. Taylor that Santa Anna had retreated. About the only thing they left on the field besides their dead and wounded was hundreds of sacks of beans.

Then they sent us eighteen miles in advance, to the Nueces, to see if Santa Anna did not stop there. About half way out we met a man on foot. It was one of Col. Bowles' men, who had been taken prisoner. They had turned him loose, and he was the proudest man I ever saw. He said he handed his gun to a Mexican officer when old Bowles ran, and the officers would not let the soldiers kill him.

We went on to the Aqua Nueva ranch. There were lots of houses there, and a great many of Santa Anna's wounded were there. One house was full of wounded. One long house full of hay was jammed with wounded. It caught fire in some way, and a good many of them were burned up.

Old Col. Churchill came on with Sherman's battery and a column of dragoons. Ben McCulloch took us back to our old camp, and while there two Mexican doctors came up with a while flag. Col. Churchill asked me to stand guard over the wounded. They had a keg of brandy. It was one of the few times in all my life that I ever felt liquor. They were operating on the wounded. At night I went to camp. Next day we all fell back to Buena Vista.

Taylor could not spare any men for guards over his wagon train. An old Mexican devil named Canales accidentally ran across three hundred of our wagons, guarded by only about fifteen men. The Mexicans butchered the guards and teamsters, burned their bodies, and burned everything. This nearly ruined us, as it left us without supplies. Even our drums had been shot all to pieces. There was not a drum in camp after the battle. Woe unto the souls of the conspirators who robbed us of our forces through political spite while we were in front of the enemy.

During the battle one company was left in the black fort. They had only one gun. Old Dominion charged the little band, but they fought like devils and stood off ten times their number during the whole day.

Peter and Mose, two free negroes, were engaged in waiting on a doctor of Bowles' regiment. Mose said to Peter, "Let's get away from here and go to the ranch." There they got under fire again. Then they started to the black fort. On the road they outran the Mexican cavalry. They said they ran to get out of one fight and got into three.

Santa Anna left without burying his dead. Gen. Taylor ordered the alcalde to send the peons to the field and bury the dead and care for the wounded. I wanted to go over the field, and I got permission. The doctors had a great knife like a carving knife. They would make the peons throw the poor wounded devils on a big box, and they would slash off the legs and arms as if they were in the butcher business. They cut one fellow's thigh off and laid him on the ground, and he died instantly, without a struggle. Such is the prose of war. One man shook him. I said, "He has vamoosed to diablo." The poor fellow began to cry. He said that the dead man was his brother. Then

I felt sorry that I had made such a remark.

By that time the Mexicans had come out from Saltillo and piled up about 700 bodies in one pile on the ridge. As I rode along the peons asked us if they could cut off the buttons. I told them yes. On the mountains I found a fine horse, with one hind leg shot off by a cannon ball. The poor thing nickered to me, but I had to ride away from him. As I came back the peons had stripped the dead, and they then scraped out a shallow place on the hillside, and barely buried them. Among the dead we found two white men—deserters, we thought.

Next day 1000 men, infantry, were put in wagons, and Bragg's and Sherman's battery followed. We advanced in pursuit of Santa Anna. We camped at the Aqua Nueva. Next day we marched on, seeing dead and wounded everywhere. McCulloch's company was in the advance. About a mile of Encarnacion we heard a noise and slowly advanced, finding a dying soldier, surrounded by his family. Our wagons carried him on to Encarnacion. He died there. A Mexican jumped on his horse in the town and fled. I was riding a fine race mare, and Ben McCulloch told me to catch him. I ran him about four miles and caught him. He had a sack of money, $333 in silver. He had a fine sword, and the fool had a good gun and it loaded. He had on the finest cloak I ever saw. He fell on his knees. I could not kill him, but he reported that I took $1500, after I had spared his life. He lied, and tried to get me into trouble.

I heard old Santa Anna's cannon; he was camped on the Salado. There were four or five hundred wounded men at Encarnacion. There were some pretty good houses, and plenty of good water, hoisted by mules.

Col. Dunlap ordered me to give up the prisoner's clothing. I gave up the cloak, and he did not say a word about the money, the horse or the sword. I have the sword yet.

Again we returned to Buena Vista. We had nothing to do. The soldiers had been paid off, and I opened a monte game.

When I closed the game I was $3000 winner.

I captured a suspicious looking character, who had the finest horse I ever saw. He was on his road to San Luis Potosi. He had in his possession a great deal of information concerning us. Gen. Woll kept the horse. He sent for a rich man named old Tom Sansome, and I think the prisoner was finally released. He seemed to have been in the employ of Sansome.

Old Capt. Walker, of an Ohio company, who was killed in the battle, was buried close to my tent. One of my tent pins stuck in his grave for three months. They took up the body to send it home, and the skin was not broken anywhere. We gave a Mexican 50 cents to wash him off, and he looked as natural as he did the day he was killed.

While scouting I found some of Santa Anna's men who had been dead for three months. I would set them up against the cactus, and they looked to be alive. The air in that country is so pure that bodies simply dry up and never decay. I went rabbit hunting one day, and I found one of the Arkansas boys looking as natural as life. He had been killed during the battle. I went up to where the Mexicans had buried their dead. It was an awful sight. The wind had blown the dirt off of the bodies, and the action of the sun had drawn the hands of the dead towards the sky. They all looked as if they were lying on their backs imploring their God. The bodies had not decayed.

In about three months Gen. Taylor received news of the victories of Gen. Scott's army around and in the City of Mexico. We were disbanded, and I took eight men and returned to Texas. We had lost about 250 dead and about 300 wounded. Gen. Taylor ordered the wounded put in one of the finest churches I ever saw, and told the old priest to keep away. It was a magnificent building, and it nearly killed the old priest to see it desecrated by the "Americano diablos." We kept it in possession about three months, and turned it over to the old priest. He rang the bells for joy two weeks, day and night, to get the influence of the heretics out of the church. He was a fine old devil.

Chapter XXII.

OPPOSES THE CIVIL WAR, BUT FINALLY ENLISTS AS A SOLDIER IN THE SOUTHERN ARMY.

Gen. Taylor doubtless heard a great deal of talk about the fine sword I had captured, and he sent for it. He sent it back to me with orders not to take the sword of an officer of the enemy unless the officer himself surrendered it.

We had rest and peace after we returned from Mexico, until the devil broke loose in the United States many years later. Emigrants had poured into the State, and under the white wings of peace everybody under the Lone Star prospered. We were congratulating ourselves that we had the finest country on earth, and that it would be easy for all of us to transmit large landed estates and plenty of cattle and horses to our children, when our congressman returned home talking of war. That disturbed us all a great deal. Old Sam Houston said it was all wrong, but the younger element overpowered him and forced the State out of the Union. I did not believe in slavery, and there were thousands just like me, but there was nothing left for us to do but shoulder arms and join our old comrades. I voted for the Union. I opposed secession. It was a terror to me to be torn from the flag I had been born under, and which I had fought under. At last, my sympathies all being with our people, I enlisted in the army. We formed a camp on the Salado. While in camp, Gen. Ben McCulloch came along, and we had a long talk. He was on his way to the States. He grasped my hand and said, "Good-bye, Hall; I will never see you again; I will never live through this war." The next I heard of him he had been killed at Pea Ridge, in Arkansas.

We elected old Dr. Woods colonel of our regiment. He is still alive. Our lieutenant colonel was named Benton, and a lawyer named Hutchinson was elected major. I joined W.L. Foster's company. He was a brother-in-law of mine. We drank a good deal of whisky in that camp. There was a Baptist preacher named Jason Ivry who helped us. I could hear him praying very loud every night. One night I went to his tent. He said he would drink me a toast. This is it:

> "The Presbyterian preaches for money,
> The Methodist preaches for cattle,
> The Baptists preach for the good of the soul,
> And they take their pay out of the bottle."

He never drank again, though he served through the whole war. He was a good man.

We next camped at San Marcos. We scouted about on the frontier for a year before we went to the army. We were down on old Caney for a short time. We were ordered to protect the country about Powder Horn and Port Lavaca. The enemy came in and captured Fort Saluria, and we fell back again on old Caney. They shelled us a great deal. This was a bit of strategy to keep us there while Gen. Banks attempted to conquer the Red River country.

We again moved over on the Brazos, close to a sugar house. A lot of the boys got on the good side of the negroes, and they told us there were two barrels of rum hid under some sugar cane. They mounted guard upon the old guard an hour before the time was on. Our boys, as soon as the guard went away, took ropes and captured the two barrels of rum. I walked out among the houses late in the evening and saw a man lying on the ground. I thought his brains had been kicked out by a horse. I told Capt. Foster about it. The man's name was Bill Pierce. Foster shook him, and I ran after Dr. Blakemore. He had simply been unloading rum from his stomach. They got him up.

While we were out West after deserters, Col. Woods was ordered to Red River. We overtook the column before it reached its destination. When we got there the great battles of Mansfield and Pleasant Hill were over.

We had great material in the West to form an army, but there never was a general in the West capable of organizing an army. They were all brave enough, but we soon saw that the officers did not know how to keep such any army together. We had plenty of brave leaders, but were unfortunate in our commanders. Few men at the head of the Confederate armies west of the Mississippi ever displayed more than ordinary military ability. A great commander in the West would have crushed everything and made the North tremble at any time during the war.

Our army was divided, and part of it sent after Gen. Steel. They let him slip away after the battle at Jenkin's Ferry. Gen. Banks fell back and fortified at Grand d'Ecore. He had a fleet of gunboats. We failed to attack him, and he fell back down the river, then took up the line of march back down Red River the way he had come. We followed. They had had a little skirmish, and I saw our people packing off our two or three dead. They were the first dead men I saw in that war.

It was rich country—a great cotton growing country. There were lots of slaves there. Gen. Banks swept the negroes as he went, both ways, and enlisted them in his army as soldiers. We could tell when he made a move by the smoke of the ruins about his columns. He set fire to everything—residences, corn cribs, and smoke houses. He was marching along old Caney, one of the richest regions in the world.

At the Peach Orchard we had a big gun we called the Bull battery. We slipped pretty close, and shelled the enemy's camp for a long time, but they never replied. Just at daylight they turned loose, and it rained bullets and cannon balls. Shells and grape fell thick. They ordered us to run into the peach orchard. I got inside. I saw some men killed in there. I said to the lieutenant, John Nixon, "This won't do," and we fell back to a little ditch. When we got to where we had left a fellow to hold our horses we found he had let them loose. I found my horse. My gunstock was bursted by a bullet. We saved our battery, but that was the hottest affair I ever witnessed. I was so tired I could not get on my horse, and I sat down by a tree to rest. While there a cannon ball came along and throwed mud all over me. I jumped on old Spot and ran out of the rain of those cannon balls. I saw a man running in a pond of water. It happened to be Drew Caraway, one of our men. I ran to him and asked him to get up behind me. A shell passed along and struck a tree near us and exploded. We turned a little out of the line of fire and reached camp in safety.

We rested there some time, and the Yankees fell back towards Alexandria. We saw them catch an old citizen, a rich planter, and rob him of all he had in his pockets. Negroes ran away in gangs, following the Federal army. I found an old negro woman in the woods, as blind as a bat. I asked her what she wanted to go with the Yankees for. She said that all her people had gone. I told her I would do her a favor—to take hold of my rope, and I would lead her into the road. She did so, and when I directed the old thing towards a house she gave me ten thousand thanks. At the crossing of Caney they threw out many loads of negro plunder.

Chapter XXIII.

BATTLE WITH THE GUNBOATS ON RED RIVER.

Col. Tom Green, a brave soldier, asked permission to fight the gunboats, and it was granted. Some man betrayed his plans to the enemy. I think there were two iron-clads and one wooden boat. At that point the river was pretty narrow, and the Federals planted sharpshooters among the trees on the other side. The river was so low it was impossible for the gunners on the gunboats to depress many of their largest guns so as to strike an enemy at short range.

Green and his men charged right up to the bank. The gunboats amounted to nothing, but the bullets began to rain from the sheltered position on the opposite shore. Our men began to fall like leaves in autumn. Gen. Green was killed right in front. As soon as he fell a retreat was ordered. They fell back to the main army.

The gunboats had had enough, and they floated down to Alexandria. The river was getting very low . We pursued them and turned out on a high hill, called McNutt's Hill. There we had a skirmish. Bank's whole army was at Alexandria, about ten miles away. Next morning Wood's regiment was dismounted, and we advanced towards Alexandria and turned into the canebrake. There we had a considerable battle with the enemy's cavalry. We drove them back. In the evening we returned to camp. That same evening the Federals took possession of some large, fine houses on a bayou. Again we gave them a fight and forced them back. Here I saw an act that would have disgraced Comanche Indians. A lot of blue-coats set fire to a fine house and dragged a woman out and left her on the grass, almost naked. One fine house had a lot of hogs near it. They set fire to it, and we could hear the poor hogs squealing. That was one of the richest, finest countries I ever saw. The Federal army left desolation and smoking ruins in their wake. No Comanches, in their raids in Texas, had ever butchered, plundered, murdered, and burned as the Federals did on that retreat.

We rested at McNutt's camp two or three days. Two or three regiments, ours included, under the command of Gen. Bee, made a circuitous march to get into Bank's front. We went around through the pine woods and halted twelve miles below Alexandria. There was a fine plantation there, and we camped there. About half a company of Yankees rode right into our camp, and we captured them.

We had some artillery, and the boys slipped up the river and captured a transport. It contained supplies and mail for the Federal army. The boys had great times laughing over the letters of the enemy.

As we marched we passed through a large negro quarter. I never saw but one old gray-headed negro man and one hog. The hog would have weighed 400 or 500 pounds. We again returned to camp. In about ten days I was on another scout, and passed by the same ranch, and I did not see the old negro. I went to the hog pen and found the hog dead. People were terribly excited. All who could get away were leaving the country.

We retreated to Marksville, on the south side of Red River. There we had a fight with the gunboats. There were some wooden gunboats, and we noticed one of these in front. We ran a battery close to the shore, and sent twenty-four shots through her. The iron-clad turned broadside and cleared the woods. They had some great guns. The balls would strike great trees and burst them into splinters.

We fell back to Marksville. From there we saw the black smoke of Alexandria, which was on fire. Banks, the Comanche of the Federal army, was at his deviltry again. He burned every town, every house and everything that he could possibly destroy in his mad retreat. Right when he was doing all this he had two men to our one and forty times as much artillery. Still he retreated and acted the vandal. Will history dare to call such a monster of iniquity and imbecility a general? We were about 5000, and some one reported the Federal advance as 40,000 strong.

We stood our ground and fought their whole army with musketry and again fell back to Manchula, seven or eight miles from Marksville. There we made a stand. Capt. Foster's company was located right in the town and we dug rifle pits with our Bowie knives. There I witnessed the greatest artillery duel I ever saw. I think they had about eighty pieces. We had twenty or twenty-five. It lasted an hour, and the earth trembled beneath the roar of the guns. We were ordered to fall back. We were still in Banks' front. I had two big, heavy six-shooters. We all jumped and ran. As I arose I knocked one of my guns out of the scabbard. I had gone fifty yards, and said to the captain, "I have lost one of my pistols." He told me to run back and get it. I replied, as the shells shrieked over our heads, "I don't think I want it." We ran about a mile. The artillery fire had slackened. I was much fatigued. I sat down by the side of a tree. My tongue had swelled. The adjutant came along and shouted, "Fall in here, Hall." I replied, "I would not do it to save your life. I have fought and run until my tongue is swollen, and I can hardly get my breath." When I got rested I joined the ranks. We went to the burnt bridge. It was burning then.

Next day they were advancing against us, and we turned into the hills. We saw the black cloud of smoke rising from the ruins, and we knew Comanche Banks was retreating again. The Federal army passed along and again got in our front. We then attacked them in the rear at Morrisville, and had a pretty heavy fight. They shelled up terribly. I got thrown from my horse.

The horse was so badly scared that I could not mount him. I got mad and sat down against a tree and said, "D—n you, shoot as much as you please." They must have shot fifty shots at me. The old horse got quiet, and I finally mounted him and rode away.

Banks commenced burning again; nothing was spared. At Yellow Bayou we concluded to make a stand. We placed the Bull battery close to the walls of an old sugar house. About 9 o'clock old Polignac's division came up on foot. They rested, and then went on in the battle. The battle raged with terrific fury all day, and we held our position. The Yankee army moved to Atchafalaya for the protection of their gunboats and transports. Next day some of Foster's men, with Capt. Holmes' men, were sent out on a scout. We reached a house, and we saw a lot of ambulances. Capt. Holmes climbed up in a tree to get a good look. Instantly they fired a big gun at us. The shell bursted in the house. Capt. Holmes did not come out of the tree; he fell out. We mounted our horses under fire and returned to headquarters and reported. They sent us out again, but I never saw another Yankee. We then buried our dead and marched to where Banks embarked his army on his river boats. Here our boys lost the old Bull gun that had done us so much service. They attacked a gunboat with her, and a monster ball, or shell, struck her exactly in the muzzle and disabled her forever.

Our army appeared to melt away. Regiment after regiment went away. I carried an express to Alexandria, to headquarters. I returned, and we were ordered to Alexandria, then to Black river, in charge of a herd of beeves. We crossed about 1000 head. They milled on us. A gunboat came up and fired on us. A big limb, cut off by a cannon shot, fell close to my head. The boys on the other side of the river got the cattle all right and got away with them.

At another time we started with 700 beeves. Just as we

crossed Black river we got news that 400 negroes were marching to attack us. We turned and recrossed. The negroes came up. My horse bogged down; I got him out. About the time I got in my saddle the negroes opened fire. The firing grew very heavy. I looked about and saw that my whole company was gone. One man named Pierce stayed with me for a while. The ground about the old gin house was covered with blankets. I thought to gather up a dozen or more, but the whole company opened fire on me and filled my face full of splinters. My horse broke loose and ran off. The boys saved the whole drove of beeves, but they left me in the closest place I had ever been in all my life. I retreated on foot. My horse had caught up with the column, and the boys rode back and met me. We ought to have fought these negroes, but we never did.

I got a furlough and came home. I told my friends I was satisfied that we were not strong enough to fight the North. We were fighting our own people, our negroes, and recruits from every country in Europe. I foresaw that the end had come, and that the sooner peace was made the better for us. We were already beaten, and ought to have stopped the war long before we did. It was the old story of the guard at Waterloo, who, when he saw the enemy's lines, took off his hat and simply said, "There are too many."

Robert Hall's gravesite in the King Cemetery near Belmont, Texas

Chapter XXIV.

RECOLLECTIONS OF MEN AND OLD TIMES.

The story of the war between the States has been told and retold on thousands of pages. Historians will not cease to write about it for centuries. It was a war I did not like, nor do I like to write of my service in it. Let it suffice for my descendants to know that I served as a soldier in that great war, and did my duty as a soldier, as I did in all other wars. That will be enough for them to remember of me in that fratricidal struggle. The negroes were not to blame; it was our war.

I will close my book with a chapter of recollections of matters that have escaped me while dictating the book.

One Capt. Taylor, who was said to be related to Gen. Taylor, fought with great bravery at Buena Vista. After the battle it is said that he found about forty old Mexican Hidalgos at Aqua Neva, and that he had them shot. He was court-martialed, and I saw him sent to the rear. He was crying. It was said that he was a brave man and aspired to high military honors.

Two soldiers went down on the San Juan and robbed an old priest of $10,000. Gen Taylor found it out, and he sent them to New Orleans to be tried. One died. The other got back on the Colorado to old Wash Secrets. He took sick and died. On his death-bed he told Old Wash that they buried the ten thousand in gold at the root of a pecan tree, thirty steps from Walnut springs, on the camp of Buena Vista. After the fellow was dead, Old Wash went to Mexico to search for the money.

He went to the field of Buena Vista, but Old Taylor had cut down all the trees to make the Black fort bomb proof. There was nothing there but stumps. He searched many days, but never found the gold. It is there yet.

LIST OF MY GENERALS AND CAPTAINS

Gen. Sam Houston, Gen. Felix Huston, Gen. Rusk, Gen. Ed Burleson, Col. Moore, Maj. Billingsley, Col. Jack Hays, Gen. Ben McCulloch, Henry McCulloch, Old Capt. Paint Caldwell, Capt. Walker, Capt. Crump, Capt. Gillespie, Capt. Jim Bird, and Capt. Callahan, one of Fannin's men.

Col. John G. King's family: William P. King, his son, fell at the Alamo. I, Robert Hall, married his daughter Polly. I married her twice and buried her twice, and never was divorced. There were eleven in the family of Col. King. All are dead but old Robert Hall. I am the only one of all these people and officers alive. I helped to take San Antonio three times. I have fought the faithful fight, and am ready for the Master's call. All I claim is seven feet of Texas soil and rest beneath the skies after life's fitful fever is over.

REMINISCENCES.

Since the close of our war, a band of Mexicans and Indians made a raid across the Rio Grande and attacked the settlement on the Weaver flat. They killed Capt. Jordan's son, and stole a good deal of property; but that was the last raid the Mexicans ever made into Texas.

Some years ago my sons captured a leopard. I made a strong cage and exhibited it at the fair in Austin, where I made considerable money. I took it to Houston. Forepaugh happened to be there. He said it was the finest specimen of the animal kingdom he ever saw, and he gave me $80 for the leopard. I called her Mary Bell. Somehow I have always regretted that I parted with the fine animal.

I think the finest part of Texas is the country about Carrizo Springs. It is a well watered country, with the finest climate on earth. There are fine flowing wells and magnificent lakes everywhere. A beautiful never-failing stream runs right through the town. Artesian water can be found at from 60 to 200 feet anywhere near the town. The soil is rich, and if irrigated would produce the finest crops in the world.

I moved to the Weaver flat, on the Nueces, and drove my cattle there after the Civil War. All the cattle drifted into the thickets of the Nueces. During the war there had been no marking and branding, and the herds had increased wonderfully. Old Jime Lowe owned nearly all the ranches. It became a common thing for a man to go out and brand these wild cattle and kill a calf whenever they wanted it. My boys had a negro boy. He went out and roped a 2-year-old bull and tied him to a tree. I hunted wild animals. The boys told me about the bull. Twenty days after he roped the bull I heard my hounds baying something, and when I came up it was the negro's bull. I cut him loose. He went a hundred yards and fell and never got up.

We made considerable improvement on the land and we had to herd our cattle. Lowe told us of a pasture at the Indian Bend, in Dimmit county. We traded for this pasture. About fifteen of us went up there and did very well. There I lost my wife. I became a wild man then. I lived in the woods and hunted. Robert went up to New Mexico and looked at the country and he concluded to go up there. I bought 500 fine goats and took them up there. At Carrizo I met one Dr. Jones, who was in the last stages of consumption. He had killed a Federal officer in

Louisiana and fled to South America. He changed his name and came back. He wanted to go with me and drive my hack. We stopped twenty-one days at Devil's river. I did all I could for this man, for he was a clever fellow. He died right there, while I was waiting for my son to come up with his cattle. I took his body back to Del Rio and buried it. I afterwards sent his trunk to his people in Louisiana.

DEATH AND BURIAL OF CAPT. PAINT CALDWELL.

About six months after the battle of Salado, brave old Capt. Caldwell, worn out with fatigue but covered with wounds and honors, sickened and died at Gonzales. He was buried under all the honors of war.

I was a member of the first grand jury that ever assembled in Gonzales. We only had one little puncheon house. Judge Jones held court in this house. A man in town had about one-half barrel of whiskey in his grocery—a small puncheon house covered with boards and weight-poles to hold the boards down. He had a puncheon for his counters and a tin cup for his customers to drink out of. When the court empannelled us the sheriff put us in the grocery. We took kindly to the half barrel of whiskey and knocked the head in, and long before morning there was not a drop of whiskey in the barrel. We tore the poor man's house down, and when called into court we reported that we could find no bills, that the people of Gonzales county had committed no offenses against the law. The court dismissed us.

Chapter XXV.

SOMETHING ABOUT MY COMRADES.

I was for a long time well acquainted with Gen. Ed Burleson. We served together in many campaigns against the Indians, and I always regarded him as one of the greatest of all our commanders. I think he and Old Paint Caldwell were two of the greatest Indian fighters that ever lived. Had it not been for the vigilance and courage of Gen. Burleson, the ever-watchful and treacherous Comanches would have burned Seguin. His long service on the frontier had made him familiar with all the customs and methods of warfare of these terrible enemies of the settlers. One of the greatest services he ever rendered his country was his short campaign against the Mexicans, Cherokees and negroes, under the infamous Cordova. This terrible butcher, at the head of a considerable force, was passing along the frontier, en route to Old Mexico, and, judging from the depredations he had already committed, it was his intention to burn the town of Seguin and murder the inhabitants. Gen. Burleson hurriedly gathered about him eighty frontiersmen and fell upon Cordova's land pirates when they were within three miles of the town. The battle opened just a little before sundown, and although it lasted but a few moments the victory of the Texans was complete. Both sides fought with great fury, but Gen. Burleson's good generalship and the valor of his comrades prevailed over the desperation of the enemy. Ten of the enemy were killed, two were wounded, and one giant of a negro taken prisoner. This ferocious monster swore at us, and raved like a pirate. He ground his teeth in rage, and declared that he would fight us as long as water ran and grass was green. We tried him before a court-martial and shot him at once. Cordova fled around Seguin, and in the night he fired on some of Caldwell's minutemen and wounded Milford Day. John Nichols, who was with Day, sprang into the river and staid all night.

Gen. Burleson had other elements of character besides valor worthy of admiration. He found a wounded Mexican soldier on the battlefield, who had been shot through the bowels, and he dismounted and lifted the poor fellow into his saddle and allowed him to ride into Seguin, while the magnanimous general walked by his side. No general was ever recognized by his men with more confidence and admiration than this same Ed Burleson. In private life he was a noble, generous, upright, honorable man.

Capt. Howard was one of my old comrades whose name does not appear sufficiently often in Texas history, but his long and courageous service in defense of his country is deserving of honorable mention. He was always ready to mount his horse and go in pursuit of the Indians, and when we were fortunate enough to overtake them this brave man was ever foremost in battle. He was very popular. Capt. Howard happened to be in command upon that memorable occasion when a lot of Indian chiefs were killed in San Antonio. He and Old Paint Caldwell— one with his sword and the other with an ax—doubtless enjoyed the opportunity to wreak a terrible revenge and punish the treachery of these red devils, who had the audacity to demand seven dollars per head for the few wretched prisoners whom they had not butchered.

Gallant, magnificent Jack Hays! Historians never tire of praising his patriotism and courage. He was all that has been said of him, and more. He loved a brave man and pitied a coward. At the battle of the Salado his coolness inspired the faltering, and his presence was worth a regiment. When the command of the army was offered to him he was too generous to take it from Old Paint Caldwell. "Any of us," he said, "can command Texans. All they ask is to be shown the road to the enemy's camp." So much faith did all of us have in the military ability of this extraordinary man that any half dozen veterans would have followed him in a charge against the whole Mexican army.

Big Foot Wallace

BIG FOOT WALLACE

THE MOST FAMOUS OF ALL THE OLD INDIAN FIGHTERS
AND VETERANS OF THE MEXICAN WAR. HE WAS A MIER
PRISONER, AND DREW A WHITE BEAN.

The name of Big Foot Wallace has been a household word on the frontier of Texas for more than sixty years. The school histories of the Lone Star State have made the children of three or four generations familiar with his eventful career in the service of his country. Gray haired comrades, enfeebled by wounds and age, sit by the fireside on wintry evenings and never tire of repeating to their descendants who are playing at their knees the history of his deeds of valor in the mountain passes and on the plains of Mexico. Though an octogenarian, the old patriot and warrior is still living in a little town in Frio county which has been named in his honor. His bearing and address is that of a man who has carried the enthusiasm of youth into old age, and his eyes kindle with a martial fire as he moves restlessly about, never happier than when engaged in telling stories of old wars and desperate hand-to-hand encounters with savage Comanches. He lived in camp for more than half a century, and during all of this time he was one of the trusted and faithful guardians of the frontier, never in a better humor than when there was a call for men of his kind to mount and go in pursuit of the enemy. He was one of the famous prisoners of Mier, and though fortunate enough to draw a white bean at the Hacienda Salado, where Santa Anna had ordered every tenth man to be shot, he was the most courageous and desperate of all that desperate band of Spartan Texans who daily challenged their trembling guards to mortal combat. Far from home, and surrounded by an army, this masterful martial spirit whispered to his comrades that he saw a ray of hope, and from their eyes sparkled a look that meant "Lead on, old Spartacus!" The next instant the Texans, with a yell that shook the earth, and with no other weapons than their hands, rushed upon a company of Mexican cavalry that had been left to guard them and unhorsed them to a man. Seizing the weapons of their conquered foes, they mounted and riding down everything that opposed them, they fled to the mountain passes. In all the wars of the world few such deeds of desperate heroism have come within the knowledge of the great chroniclers of events.

In the gloomy dungeons of Perote it took seven giant Mexicans to throw this struggling Texan to the earth and bind him. After he had lain fourteen days chained hand and foot, face downwards, to a rock, without food or water, when the thongs were cut and the rivets forced apart, his first act was to spring at one of his tormenters and try to throttle him.

Now, at the age of eighty-one, while strong in body and mentally vigorous, though he trembles with a palsy that resulted from the tortures inflicted in the dungeons of Perote, he says the government insults him by offering a disgrace pension of $8 per month. "This is a disgrace," says the old soldier, "from the fact that the army that conquered Mexico won the greatest extent of territory that was ever wrung from a defeated nation in any one war. We gained a whole empire—doubled the territory of the country, and moved the western boundaries from the valley of the Mississippi beyond the gold fields of California, to the shores of the Pacific."

William Alexander Anderson Wallace, who has been known throughout the whole of the United States for more than half a century as "Big Foot" Wallace, was born near Lexington, Va., in Rockbridge county, in 1817.

He comes of good old Revolutionary stock, many of his

father's kinsmen having served in Washington's army. Wallace's father was too young to be a soldier, and his brothers, who had volunteered to fight the British, persuaded him to remain at home and take care of the women and children. Several of Wallace's ancestors were slain in battle, and some of them were buried in the old cemetery near Lexington. The family claimed to have descended from the fighting Wallaces of Scotland, and those who have seen old Big Foot leading a charge in battle declare that they needed no further evidence as to the correctness of this historical statement.

When Mr. Wallace arrived in Texas the War of Independence had about ended. Santa Anna was a prisoner, and it was believed that a permanent peace would soon be established between Texas and Mexico. The army had been collected in the eastern part of the Republic for the purpose of fighting the Mexicans, and as a consequence the frontier was very poorly protected. The Comanches and other wild hostile tribes took advantage of this condition of affairs and raided the settlements at their pleasure. It was not long, however, before the commander of the army—who was no less important a character than Albert Sidney Johnston—could spare a force to meet these red devils and punish their audacity with sword and fire. Big Foot Wallace at once enlisted and served for many years with these frontier troops, and it was not long before he was known on the border as one of the most daring and desperate Indian fighters on the plains. He was always in front, always anxious to lead a charge, and in battle he demanded the post of danger. If there was any hard riding to do or any spying or dangerous scouting to execute in the enemy's country, such brave officers as Jack Hays and Old Paint Caldwell knew exactly where to find the man who was in every way capacitated for such work. In one of these dangerous expeditions Mr. Wallace came nearly losing his life. He was crawling along a ledge of rock by the side of a bluff not far from Austin. There was barely room for him to walk along the ledge, which was far above the stream that was roaring and splashing below him. He came to a projecting rock and peeped cautiously around it. It so happened that a big Comanche warrior, who had evidently been watching Wallace, peeped from the other side of the projection at the same instant. The faces of the two enemies, bitter with hatred and kindled by two pairs of eyes burning with rage, were not six inches apart. Both men drew their weapons for battle on that narrow ledge, with no witnesses but the eagles. Wallace was the quicker of the two, and just as the Indian's arrow appeared around the rock the gun of the Texan cracked in the warrior's face and his body rolled, bounding from ledge to ledge, into the torrent below, while the eagles shrieked a requiem.

In September, 1842, when the Mexican General Woll made a dash into Texas and surprised and captured San Antonio, Wallace was serving with the famous Jack Hays. This company of gallant horsemen were first in the enemy's front, and formed a rallying point for the army that almost instantly assembled under Gen. Matthew Caldwell. Hays was ordered to select a battle ground, and he met the enemy at Salado. Here a pitched battle was fought between 300 Texans and 1500 Mexicans, and the enemy were driven from the field with great slaughter. This was one of the greatest victories ever won by the army of Texas, and the Republic was indebted to the individual bravery of the rank and file for all the glory of that memorable day. Big Foot Wallace was everywhere, sometimes firing a musket, and at others slashing the enemy with a great bowie knife. The example of his valor amongst the whistling bullets was worth a whole regiment. After the great victory Col. Jack Hays put his hand on Wallace's shoulder and said, "Here is a soldier whom Napoleon would have made a marshal of France. He has demonstrated that there are men who love a battle better than a ball, and to such men the word fear conveys no meaning."

Gen. Woll instantly commenced a hurried retreat toward

Mexico, while the Texans hung on his rear and gave him no time to rest. They constantly engaged his rear guard, and upon one occasion Jack Hays at the head of his old company charged into the Mexican camp. Had he been supported, Gen. Woll's army would have been destroyed. Gen. Somervell, who was in command of the Texans, would not pursue the Mexicans across the Rio Grande, and in pursuance of orders from the Republic he ordered a retreat. Here 300 enraged Texans, smarting under the wrongs that Santa Anna in violation of his oath had inflicted upon them, demanded to be led into Mexico that they might avenge themselves upon the merciless enemy who were guilty of the Dawson massacre, and so many other murders. William S. Fisher volunteered to lead this desperate band, and they at once elected him their general.

Embarking in boats, they floated down the Rio Grande to the Mexican town of Mier. The Alcalde surrendered the town and the Texans retired to their camp to await a supply of provisions which the Alcalde had promised to collect. On December 25th, the Texans discovered that Gen. Ampudia, at the head of an army of 2000 men, was in possession of Mier. They at once prepared to give him battle. Big Foot Wallace says this was the hardest fought battle that he ever witnessed. The Texans forced a passage across the river in the face of a rain storm of musket balls and a galling shower of grape and canister. They dashed along a street in the darkness, for the battle was fought before daylight, drove the Mexican infantry before them and captured a group of store houses near the plaza. When morning broke the Mexicans turned their cannon upon the buildings occupied by the Texans. Big Foot Wallace with two or three riflemen devoted their attention to these cannon. At the first fire they knocked down every gunner. Three times the Mexicans manned the guns, and as many times the unerring marksmen destroyed them. As the cannon were dragged away the Texans could see that the wheels were red with blood.

Mexican infantry swarmed on the housetops and rained bullets through every opening upon the Texans. The riflemen of the frontier were at home in this kind of warfare, and while a constant blaze of fire poured from their shelter the Mexicans could be seen falling upon the roofs of the houses and their blood ran from the gutters in a stream. Time and again Mexican officers with gallant daring led columns of infantry against the store house, but the Texans repulsed them with ease. During the day Gen. Fisher was badly wounded, and it was while he was lying on the floor writhing in agony that something happened that has never been explained. Every Texan was feeling confident of victory, when a white flag appeared. Gen. Ampudia informed Gen. Fisher that a reinforcement of 1700 Mexican regulars were about to arrive on the field. He spoke of the bravery of the Texans in the highest terms of praise, and pledged his honor to grant them the most honorable terms if they would surrender, but he told them that they must not expect any quarter if they held out until the arrival of the regulars. Half of the soldiers did not know what was going on, and when they found that there was talk of surrendering they surrounded Capt. Cameron and Big Foot Wallace and demanded that these two should lead them in a forlorn hope if necessary. After Cameron and Wallace had made some observations they discovered that a strong column of Mexican infantry with several pieces of artillery occupied the field between the position of the Texans and the river. Only a few knew the true state of affairs when the terms of surrender had been completed. Many cried like children when they gave up their weapons. They afterwards learned that Ampudia had determined to retreat when an officer suggested the idea of tricking Gen. Fisher into surrendering. The Texans were to be kept on the border and "treated with the consideration which is in accordance with the magnanimous Mexican nation." Big Foot Wallace shouted to Fisher in a rage, "Mexican magnanimity means to fill a prisoner with boiled beans one day and bullets the next."

The prisoners were at once started on a long march towards the dungeons of Perote, where they knew they would be tortured to death. At the Hacienda Salado they overpowered a company of cavalry, and taking the arms and horses from the trembling wretches they rode away in a gallop. Had they kept the great highroad, they could easily have marched straight to Texas, but a few shouted, "To the mountains!" Cameron and Wallace realized the mistake, but fearing the Texans might get separated they left the road. There were 193 of them. Enough to have whipped a whole Mexican army. It was not long before they were hopelessly lost and entangled in the mountain passes. Days passed and they saw no sign of a road or a human habitation. The weak began to perish of hunger and thirst. Brave soldiers rode along in speechless agony, with their tongues hanging black and parched from their cracked lips. Some became insane and rushed wildly about scratching into the earth for water. A few killed their horses, and others sucked the blood from the veins of the poor staggering beasts. Many threw away their arms and bid their comrades farewell. Big Foot Wallace possessed such a splendid physical constitution that he was able to endure it all and his mind never wandered. When the noble hearted Col. Mexia came upon the poor unfortunates, Wallace was about the only one able to speak. The wretched condition of the wanderers and the piteous appeals in their eyes touched the heart of the generous and brave Mexia, and he at once ordered his soldiers to give the prisoners their canteens of water and their rations. Noble Mexia! His name will ever be held sacred in the hearts of the children of the old Texans, and they have named a pretty town in his honor.

Incredible as it may appear, nine of these prisoners reached Texas. The remainder were returned to the Hacienda Salado and all heavily ironed. Santa Anna ordered Col. Mexia to shoot every tenth man, but this brave soldier replied that "he would have nothing to do with such an inhuman piece of butchery."

A wretch was easily found who executed the massacre. One hundred and fifty-nine white beans and seventeen black ones were placed in an earthen mug and the prisoners drew for life or death. Mr. Wallace says that it has often been reported that he offered to exchange his white bean with a poor fellow who was crying. This story is not true. The Mexican butcher, who seemed to be enjoying the bloody affair, would not permit any trading. Capt. Cameron drew life, but when Santa Anna heard of it, he said, "I will show the lucky dog that I am stronger than fate," and he ordered him shot. The brave Scot went to death with his eyes unbandaged and a smile on his face, as if he were on his way to a festival or a battle.

There is a remarkable story connected with this affair which Big Foot Wallace vouches for. A man by the name of Sheppard drew a black bean and he was shot with the other condemned men. Sheppard fell, but he instantly realized that he was not fatally shot. He lay perfectly still and showed no signs of life while the assassins were stripping him naked and dragging him to the heap of slain. That night Sheppard crawled from among the dead bodies of his comrades, and though perfectly naked he ran many miles. Mr. Wallace says that he has heard that this poor fellow wandered about over the rocks and among the cactus for five days and nights. He finally reached a house and threw himself upon the mercy of the Mexican rancher. It would most certainly have been a merciless wretch who would not have been moved to pity by this man's miserable condition. His feet were bleeding and his flesh had been torn by cactus; his eyes were bloodshot and his tongue parched. The Mexican hid him under the floor of his house and promised to take him to Texas. The grave diggers had counted the bodies, and finding one missing they reported the fact. The lancers trailed the poor fellow to his hiding place by the blood he had left on the rocks, and they dragged him out and shot him at once.

The prisoners were ironed and many were thrown into gloomy dungeons. Upon one occasion some ladies came to see them and they wept over the fate of the poor Americans. One fine lady said to the guards. "Why do you keep these poor men ironed? Are you afraid of them?" The reply was, "It is the Governor's orders."

"Well," she exclaimed, "I am the wife of the Governor, and I intend to cut these chains." She went away and returned in a few moments with a blacksmith and she made him cut the irons off all of us . I was ironed again, with fourteen others. On the fifth day they began to die. One lasted until the twelfth. I have forgotten his name. On the fourteenth day the British minister and a surgeon general in the Mexican army came into the prison, and the Mexican officer cut the cords on my arms and ordered the chains unlocked. He and the Briton were cursing about the inhumanity of the officers of the prison when the prison doctor came in and the Mexican officer drew his sword and beat him all over the room. These two men spoke with unutterable contempt of the American minister in Mexico, who had made no effort to ameliorate our condition. The surgeon general dressed my wounds and greatly admired my form, and when he learned that I had been bound on my face for fourteen days, he said to British minister, "He is certainly one of the finest specimens of physical manhood that I ever saw." He asked what I could eat, and I replied, "A wolf." Both of them laughed. Soon afterwards a boy appeared with a good dinner, and while I was eating, the villain who had bound me appeared. I immediately sprang at his throat and would have throttled him if they had not overpowered me. That terrible experience brought on a stroke of palsy which afflicts me to this day. There were many good women in Mexico, and the one who excelled them all in beauty and lovely attributes of mind and heart was the wife of Santa Anna. She came to see us very often and always brought us something to relieve our sufferings. She gave us all of the tobacco that we had for a long time. Often her sister or Santa Anna's sister came with her and they always spoke words of comfort and good cheer. We heard officers say that she was constantly appealing to her cruel husband to release us. On her deathbed she made him promise to send the poor Texans home, and they say that although he loved her very much that he granted her dying request with great reluctance. Two girls in a little store were our friends. They managed to get letters to our friends in Texas, and smuggled replies in loaves of bread. We got a good deal of money in loaves, and they smuggled one prisoner $800 and he divided it among us.

We were released in 1844, after having endured every species of cruelty and torture that the inhuman Mexicans could devise for about twenty-two months. A great many escaped and many others died. Of the three hundred who were at Mier, I don't think over one-half ever got back to Texas. I know of but one besides myself who is alive to-day. His name is Boone and he lives over on the Blanco.

The surviving Mier prisoners only had a few years to wait before an opportunity presented itself for them to avenge themselves upon the Mexicans. War soon afterwards broke out between the United States and Mexico. Big Foot Wallace no sooner heard the news than he mounted his horse and rode to the nearest military camp. He served with his characteristic energy and intrepidity, and behaved with such gallantry at Monterey as to win a complimentary notice from the commanding general. He belonged to Col. Jack Hays' famous regiment, but when Capt. Gillespie was killed Big Foot took command of his company. He found a cannon overturned, but noticing that it had not been spiked, he righted it and asked for a gunner. An Irishman stepped from the ranks, and with the remark that he had "sarved five years in the Queen's sarvice," he sighted the gun and put a ball through the wall of a house that the Americans wanted to possess. Big Foot helped his newly found gunner and they soon drove the Mexicans from the building. Then Big Foot charged with his company and gained possession of a strategic point. Here commenced a peculiar battle. The Americans fought from house to house and from room to room, digging through adobe walls with their bayonets, and driving the Mexicans before them through doors and windows that had been shot into sieves. The Texans were the first to gain a plaza and display the American flag from the walls.

After peace had been made Big Foot Wallace returned to Texas, intending to do a little farming and raise a herd of cattle, but the Indians would not let the people alone and he had to resume his old occupation of killing them. He followed them to their mountain fastnesses a hundred times, and skirmished with them equally as often. He fought nine pitched battles with them, beating them every time. He had been in five great battles with the Mexicans and so far had never been wounded, but in his most famous battle with the Comanches near Cotulla he was slightly wounded, and no less than seven bullets passed through his clothing, while several arrows were lodged in his buckskin coat. There were ninety-seven warriors, and Big Foot was following them with only nineteen men; but they were all trained Indian fighters, capable of taking the reins in their teeth and riding down an enemy with a revolver in each hand. A brave young chief rode boldly out on the prairie and challenged Big Foot to open the battle. He pranced about on a fine horse, shaking his lance defiantly at the Texans, and shouting "Come on, Big Foot. I know you and want your scalp." There were twenty-five warriors in full view and others concealed, but the Texans did not hesitate. The young chief charged, riding far ahead of his warriors, and urging them to use arrows. Big Foot ordered two of his best riflemen to shoot at the chief's legs, and at the crack of their guns his horse fell, but he lit on his feet with blood spurting from his hip. Big Foot had Jim Bowie's old rifle, that had been given to him by Madam Candelario, and with this famous gun he shot the chief dead. The Indians fell back, but the Medicine Man rallied them, and while swinging his magic roots over his head and singing a wild, weird song, he led them back to recover the body of their fallen chief. Big Foot instantly led his men in a wild, fearless charge. Thirteen of the warriors fell, and the remainder fled in confusion. The Texans followed them up on the Nueces and surprised their camp. A desperate battle ensued, and of the ninety-seven warriors known to have been in the raid, more than half were killed.

This broke the power of the Comanches and they never made another murdering expedition into that part of Texas. "My men always fought well," says the old veteran, "except one. At the battle of Twin Sisters he wanted to run away, and I tore off a mesquite limb and beat him over the shoulders, telling him that if he did not fall in and fight that I would kill him and save the Indians the trouble." The Lipans upon one occasion surprised Big Foot and made him a prisoner. Their chief, Juan Castro, who was one of the smartest Indians that ever lived, amused himself by bringing out a hideous old squaw and telling the prisoner that his only hope of escaping torture and death was lodged in the hands of this old woman. "You, Big Foot," said the chief, "you killed her husband in battle, and unless you take his place and marry her at once, my people will burn you alive." Big Foot gazed for a moment upon the weather-beaten, scarred visage of the monstrosity and coolly said to the chief while looking unflinchingly into his face, "Tell your people to light their fire." Castro laughed heartily. A few days afterwards Big Foot escaped and fled to his home. To his surprise, when he rode up to his gate, he found Juan Castro there to salute him. The chief stayed over night with him. He wanted to make an alliance with the Texans against the Comanches, and he induced Big Foot to go and see President Houston and execute the treaty for him. Castro and Big Foot were ever after warm friends, and when the great chief died the Lipans invited Big Foot to the funeral. The mourning warriors killed 300 horses for the service of their great chief in the happy hunting grounds.

Mr. Wallace was never married. He says that when a young man he was engaged to a very beautiful young girl in old Virginia. He was taken sick and lost all his hair, and he went into a cave in the mountains to wait until it grew out again before he presented himself to the idol of his heart. After some months he concluded that his scalp was pretty well concealed, and with hopes beating high he went straight to the home of his lady love, and arrived just in time to see her coming from the hymeneal altar, leaning on the arm of one of his old rivals. He at once started for Texas, and says that "since that time he has never had much faith in any but very young or very old women." During the late war he remained on the frontier in the service of Texas. "I wanted nothing to do with that foolish war," he says. "I did not want to see the Union dissolved, and I could not fight against old Virginia, and I would have fought a regiment before I would have shouldered a musket on either side." He could easily have been a general in the Southern army, but he would storm and foam in wrath whenever the war was mentioned.

The courage and fearlessness of this remarkable man was never more fully exemplified than in his services to the government while carrying the mails through the Indian country, between San Antonio and El Paso. Although the plains and mountain passes swarmed with hostile Comanches and Apaches, they never dared to attack Big Foot Wallace. The very first man who succeeded him in this business was captured by the Indians and mercilessly tortured. They hung him up by his legs and built a fire under his head and danced around the poor fellow until he died in horrible agony. His name was Jim Giddings.

"One very strange thing happened in one of my Indian campaigns," says Mr. Wallace, "which may interest people who believe in dreams. We left our dead on a battlefield, and at night a lady dreamed that a man by the name of Wilbarger was not dead. Our boys assured her that her nocturnal information was incorrect. They said that they saw Mr. Wilbarger fall, and plainly saw an Indian scalp him. She was not at all satisfied. After a time she awoke us, and told us that she had dreamed the same thing again. She finally declared that she knew the man was not dead, and insisted so strongly that we should return to the field that I and two or three others volunteered to go, though the country was swarming with Indians. Strangely enough, we found the man alive and crawling towards the settlements, though the scalp had been torn from his skull. He lived many years afterwards."

They call Mr. Wallace "Big Foot," and doubtless he will always be known in the history of the country by that name, though he wears a No. 6 boot, on a very shapely foot. We have the true story of the origin of this name from his own lips. He was stopping in Austin in early times at the house of a jolly old Texan by the name of Gravis. There was a half-civilized, very treacherous Indian in the country, who had a wonderful foot. It was 14 inches in length, and he weighed over 300 pounds. One day this Indian peeped into a room where there was a young girl. Mr. Gravis came home and saw the moccasin track, and he jokingly accused Mr. Wallace of peeping at the girl, "for," said he, "you are the only man about the house who wears Indian moccasins." Mr. Wallace was indignant, and he went and put his foot in the Indian's track. They all laughed a great deal, and an Irishman went up the street telling the story, and people began jokingly to address Mr. Wallace as "Big Foot." The name stuck to him, and Uncle Sam has been so much pleased with it that he has named a postoffice in his honor. The big-foot Indian was not slain in battle by Mr. Wallace, but killed in a hand-to-hand encounter by a noted Texan Indian fighter by the name of Westfall.

"The greatest of all my battles," says Mr. Wallace, "was that of Mier. There less than 300 of us killed 822 Mexicans. Gen. Morena, of Ampudias' staff, admitted this fact to me while I was a prisoner in Mexico."

Big Foot Wallace is highly honored and respected throughout the length and breadth of the Lone Star State, and the house of every old Texan is his home. He might have been a rich man, but, aside from the fact that nearly his whole life has been devoted to the service of his country, he possessed one trait of character that prevented him from accumulating any property. Liberality with him was always so conspicuous as to be a fault. He never possessed a dollar that was not at the service of a friend or any stranger in distress.

Texas is very proud of Big Foot Wallace, and when he goes to San Antonio, Galveston, or Houston he is always accorded an ovation that would flatter the President of the United States.

"I loved old Texas," he says with a sigh, "but barbed wire and locomotives have played the mischief with my country."

BRAZOS

Index